THE BRITISH HUMILIATION OF BURMA

THE BRITISH HUMILIATION OF BURMA

Terence R. Blackburn

Orchid Press
Bangkok 2000

Terence R. Blackburn
THE BRITISH HUMILIATION OF BURMA

First published 2000

© Orchid Press Books 2000

Orchid Press
P.O. Box 19
Yuttitham Post Office
Bangkok 10907, Thailand

This book is printed on acid-free long life paper
which meets the specifications of ISO 9706/1994

ISBN 974-8304-66-3

CONTENTS

PREFACE

Burma is, among the many countries colonized during the Nineteenth Century, one of the unluckiest in terms of exploitation during the past one hundred and fifty years or so. It is not that the Burmese Kings before the onset of colonial expansion amassed their wealth through peaceful means; far from it. The destruction and looting of the Mon kingdom of Pegu, of Myohaung in Arakan and of Ayuthia in Thailand, to name a few, were colossal and are well documented.

It is in many ways a puzzle how 'The Golden Country' Burma could end up as an unlucky and impoverished nation up to the present time. This book looks at the looting of Burmese wealth as a result of imperial expansion, and contributes to our understanding of what happened when the British dealt the final blow to the ancient Burmese kingdom in 1885. Mr Blackburn's study ends here.

Did this event set in motion a chain of events, that became uncontrollable?.

Burma was unceremoniously incorporated into the Indian 'Empire' and did not succeed until 1934 in gaining status as a separate colony, or dominion. During this period, Burma was exploited through many means, and served to balance the budget of the Indian colonial enterprise, with only a fraction of the taxation being re-invested in the country itself.

The Second World War resulted in Japanese occupation and further exploitation. Recent Japanese studies have shown that the post-war reconstruction of Japan was to a considerabe extent financed by huge amounts of assets taken from South-East Asian countries occupied during the war. Apparently, this was a well planned and meticulouisly executed operation. After the war, under the highest level of guidance, these funds 'somehow' found their way into the Japanese economic recovery budgets. It would be safe to assume that Burma contributed its fair share to these funds, and hence to Japan's post-war economic recovery.

Despite these and other setbacks, the able leader Aung San managed to negotiate a peaceful end to the colonial rule, and gain independence for his country and people in 1947 – only to be asassinated just before independence. A democratic Burma struggled on, until being brought under military rule in 1962, an event that ushered in an era of poor economic management and further decline in the nation's wealth. A sad and poignant reminder of this is the stream of Burmese cultural relics and important antiquities which flow steadily into neighbouring countries and subsequently on to world markets.

Is the 1886 picture on page 117 symbolic of what was to be in store for Burma and the Burmese people for the following hundred plus years?

David Murray
House Editor

LIST OF ILLUSTRATIONS

MAPS

ACKNOWLEDGEMENTS

I must begin by acknowledging all the help and encouragement I have received from Noel F. Singer and this I gladly do. I have benefitted from his knowledge and advice which was unstintingly given. He has not only translated the hitherto unpublished Burmese sources which I feel has added colour to an otherwise bland narrative, but was also responsible for the map [overleaf] and the material for the illustrations. I feel that the pudding is mine but the plums are his. However, I alone must take the responsibility for the view I have put forward and for any errors I may have made.

I have read widely during the preparation of this book and taken information from many sources, all of which I hope I have acknowledged. If I have inadvertently failed to do so I hope that the sin of omission may be forgiven with a *mea culpa* and a humble apology.

Extracts/quotations from Crown copyright documents in Oriental and India Office Collections of the British Library appear by permission of the Controller of Her Majesty's Stationery Office.

I would also like to record my thanks to the staff at Luton Library, Bedfordshire.

The majority of the illustrations are from the two leading papers *The Graphic* and *The Illustrated London News*, which covered the three Anglo-Burmese Wars with their vivid reporting and equally striking engravings; the cuttings now form part of Noel F. Singer's and my collection of photographs, prints and newspapers.

Terence R. Blackburn
Bedfordshire
1999

12

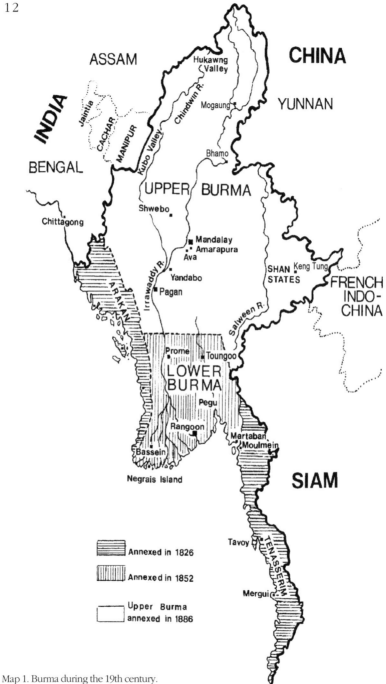

Map 1. Burma during the 19th century.

Chapter I

Introduction

Burma, now called Myanmar, has had a violent political history since the eleventh century, when the Burmese established themselves as the dominant power. Bids for supremacy involving the Arakanese, Mon and Shan produced constant anarchy. Albeit there were other lesser ethnic groups within its territories, but they were too disorganized to pose a serious threat.

Under aggressive kings with a taste for expansionist policies, the Burmese raided neighbouring kingdoms and occupied them, but were incapable of bringing them under permanent subjugation. However, during the nineteenth century the tables were turned, and the aggressors themselves became the victims of the arch empire builder – the British Raj. Three wars were fought which culminated in the once-proud nation becoming yet another appendage of Imperial India in 1886.

The intention of this book is to shed some impartial light on this period of Burmese history, the humiliation of which is still felt acutely by its people. On the one hand, it exposes the double-dealings of some of the British merchants and civil servants, together with those of a few Burmese. On the other hand, although there were attempts by far-sighted individuals on both sides to bring about a peaceful solution, they were powerless to prevent the inevitable outcome.

The book also focuses on the enigma of the fate of the fabled royal treasure that 'went missing' during the days of confusion leading up to the deportation of the King and the royal family to India. But, before proceeding, it may prove useful to review the events leading up to the fall of the last king of the Konbaung dynasty (1752-1885).

Man has occupied the land of Burma since the earliest times. Evidence has revealed that 400,000 years ago, a people who have been classified as the Anyathian (from the Burman word *ah-nyar-thar* for a man from Upper Burma) were already living in the central part of the country. In 1969, rock paintings and 1,600 stone tools claimed to be 5,000 years old, were found in the Pyadalin (shining-like-mercury) Cave, in the Shan States. In historic times the Pyu, a Tibeto-Burman race, became dominant from about 200 BC. Contemporary Chinese accounts recorded that they were agriculturists and traders who established city states within easy access to the Irrawaddy River; in the 1970s and 1980s several fortified sites were discovered. The Pyu are also known to have enjoyed maritime trade with other South-East Asian kingdoms.

Further south, the Mon, who belonged to the same racial group as the Khmer, also flourished. On the western coast, which was later to become known as Rakhaing (Arakan), an Indianized kingdom prospered, with its capital at Vaisali. In AD 832 a devastating attack was launched by the Man (Tai-Shans) of Nanzhao on Sri Kshetra, the capital of the Pyu. Next to fall was the important Mon port of Mi-ch'en in 835. While the Mon recovered, the Pyu never regained their dominance. Arakan, fortunately, was spared.

It was at about this time that another group of nomads who called themselves the Myanmar (Burmans) and who had begun infiltrating the Kyaukse regions in Upper Burma, took control of the Pyu kingdom. According to tradition, one of their chiefs established himself at Pukan (Pagan now Bagan) in 849.

The Pagan period of the Burmans (1044-1287) officially began with their first historical King, Aniruddhadeva (r.1044-77). He sacked the Mon capital Sadhuim (Thaton) in 1057 and carried off its inhabitants back to Pagan. These included artisans, monks and scholars, and it was the latter who taught their conquerors to read and write. Refinement and culture were introduced at court and the Burman never looked back. Henceforth, it became the norm for future kings with an imperialistic streak to forcibly import people of an annexed territory, to provide the manpower needed to maintain the economic, cultural and political dominance of the state.

By the thirteenth century, assisted by the Pyu, Mon and Indians (the latter refugees escaping the Muslim oppressions in India), the former riverside village of Pagan had become a great metropolis and a religious centre teeming with thousands of temples, monasteries and shrines. An attitude of tolerance prevailed, with Theravada and Mahayana Buddhism, together with Brahmanism, Hinduism, animism and other beliefs flourishing side by side. During the second half of the thirteenth century, the Burmans clashed with Khublai Khan, and the glory days of Pagan gradually came to an end. Although the encounter with the Mongols was one of the causes, another contributing factor was that through intense religious fervour, a large percentage of rich agricultural land had been donated to the Buddhist clergy. This state of affairs substantially reduced the revenues of the Crown. Further, in their relentless quest for merit and subsequent salvation, king and commoner alike diverted their surplus wealth to religion.

Power struggles between the Burman and the Shan which followed meant that political gravity shifted first to Myinsaing, followed by Pinya, Sagaing and finally settled at Inn Wa (Ava) in 1364, where a dynasty of Burmese-Shan kings ruled until 1555. Although these were unstable times, and the once united kingdom had broken up into petty states, literature and the arts flourished. It was at

Ava, in about 1435, that the Burmans had their first encounter with a European. This was Nicolo di Conti, the famous merchant of Venice who has left a vivid account of the Burman capital. Others foreigners were to follow, drawn by the fabled riches of the land. By about 1519, the Portuguese had established a trading post at the old Mon port of Muttama (Martaban).

In the sixteenth century, the Burman again came into his own at Toungoo, where under Tabinshwehti (r.1531-50) a new dynasty known as the Toungoo (1531-99) was founded. With the aid of Indian and Portuguese mercenaries, the King defeated the Mon of Hongsawathoy (Hanthawaddy in Lower Burma) and made his capital Paygo (the 'Panconia' of Nicolo di Conti) his own. The brutality and treachery of this period can best be read in the startling accounts by Fernao Mendes Pinto. Tabinshwehti's brother-in-law, Bayinnaung (r. 1551-81) enlarged his dominions by annexing the surrounding kingdoms, including Thailand. In the grand traditional manner, the cream from among the artisans were selected and taken back and the defeated soldiers were forced to drink the water of allegiance and be absorbed into the royal army. Glutted with the loot of the conquered states, Pegu became the richest and most splendid city in South-East Asia for several decades. Europeans who have left accounts of this amazing period are the Dominican friars Gaspa de Cruz and Bomferrus; Cesare Fedrici, Gaspero Balbi and the Elizabethan Ralph Fitch.

The days of glory, however, did not last. In the hands of Ngasudayaka (r.1581-99), the great empire which had been founded on oppression and savagery fragmented and much of its population was enslaved. European observers and native chroniclers alike reported that the King was an incompetent sadist who was noted for his tyrannical excesses. Pegu with its gilded palaces was burnt to the ground by invading Arakanese forces. The Jesuit, Nicholas Pimenta, writing in about 1600 has left harrowing tales of these catastrophic events.

In 1599, under Nyaungyan (r.1599-1605), the Toungoo dynasty (also known as the Nyaungyan) was restored. Although Anaukpetlun (r.1605-28) and Thalun (r.1629-48) were dynamic and able to bring order from the chaos, the kings who followed were weak and power remained in the hands of ministers. Civil wars also robbed the country of its manpower and resources became exhausted. It was at this time that the East India Company, lured by tales of profits to be made, began to show an interest in the kingdom.

By the first half of the eighteenth century, the former vassals such as the Manipuris and the Mon, sensing the weakness of the administration, broke out in revolt and ravaged the country. Indigenous accounts tell of the terrible sufferings experienced by the people at the hands of rapacious officials and the invaders. At court, corruption and drunkenness was rife. In 1742, unable to bear the oppression, thousands of Burman families fled to the neighbouring kingdom of Arakan. The Mon of Pegu declared their independence and in 1752 sacked Ava, taking back to Pegu the entire court and much treasure. The capital was torched. In that year, Aung Zeya, the headman of Shwebo, declared himself King and as Alaungmintaya (r.1752-60), founded the Konbaung dynasty (1752-1885). He fought off several Mon attacks and in 1756-57 captured Pegu. It was during his reign that the dynasty's first clash with the British occurred, when in 1759 their traders on the island of Negrais were massacred by his soldiers.

The power of the Konbaung kings reached its peak with Myedu Min (r.1763-76), who was described as an imperialist of the worst kind, and who successfully attacked the fabulously wealthy but effete kingdom of Thailand. His soldiers even managed to beat off imperial Chinese armies four times between 1766-9. The small states which suffered most under the Burmans were Assam and Manipur, for their peoples were treated with the most indescribable cruelty.

Vincenzo Sangermano, the Italian Barnabite priest, said that
it is when they enter without resistance an enemy's country that they show their true spirit; which, while it is most vile and dastardly in danger, is proportionably proud and cruel in victory. The crops, the houses, the convents of Talapoins [Buddhist monks] are all burnt to the ground, the fruit trees are cut down, and all the unfortunate inhabitants, who may fall into their hands, murdered without distinction.' Another observer noted that 'in war the men display the ferocity of savages while in peace they boast a considerable degree of gentleness and civilization'.

Under Badon Min (r. 1782-1819) the ancient kingdom of Arakan was annexed in 1784-5, and together with Assam, the Burmans now shared a common border with the British in India. With the death of Badon Min, the assertiveness of his successors weakened with each succession. The attitude at court became insular and inward looking and an extremely arrogant stance was adopted, partly due to ignorance of the outside world and its powers.

By the second half of the nineteenth century, an imperial kingdom which once stretched from Manipur in the north to the Isthmus of Kra in the south, had been shrunk dramatically by the two wars with the British in 1824-6 and 1852. Finally, in 1885 it lost its independence altogether.

The first Anglo-Burmese War was without doubt caused by the Burmese, although it appears that they had plenty of provocation. The second war had more than a hint of comic opera about it. It began as a farce and ended in tragedy. The Viceroy appointed Commodore Lambert to conduct negotiations with the Governor of Rangoon. This, however, was an unfortunate choice, for Lambert, who was nicknamed the 'Combustible Commodore', acted predictably like a bull in a china shop. Everything he did was calculated to bring about a war. The third war invited universal derision, undertaken as it was on behalf of a British commercial concern that may or may not have cheated the Burmese King and its own employees. Needless to say, after the war nothing further was heard of the matter.

By 1886 this once proud land had become just another province of the British Raj. Its former vassals would say that this was divine retribution. A people whose kings styled themselves Cakkavatti (Conqueror of the World) and who supposedly possessed the *vajiravudha* (the celestial weapon of the Hindu god Sakra), and who felt that it was their right to subjugate neighbouring kingdoms, had themselves been forced to taste their own bitter medicine – 'the biter bit'. The country was to remain part of the British Empire until 1948 when it regained its independence, after a traumatic occupation by the Japanese Imperial Army during World War Two.

I have read many books on the history of Burma, most of which have been written by Western historians and a few by Burmans. So striking is the difference between them that they could almost have been writing about different countries. I have, therefore, decided to adopt the middle ground as an impartial observer. As to the fate of the loot from the Mandalay Palace, I found it difficult to believe that so much could disappear without trace and only the parts of the regalia which were publicly known survived. There are even now millions of pounds of jewellery unaccounted for.

In *Private Affairs*, published by King Thibaw's daughter, the Fourth Princess, she asks 'where is the Crown Ruby "Nga Mauk"?' By way of answer, she recounts how when the King and Queen were about to leave Mandalay for exile in India, they secreted the jewel in their betel box. Colonel Sladen, who had been in charge of the royal party, asked if he might examine it, and they obliged. Her parents told her that after looking at it for a while, Sladen put it in his pocket, pretending to be absent-minded, and did not return it. The Princess claims a similar fate befell personal and state jewellery worth millions of pounds which were handed to Sladen for 'safe keeping'. Bearing in mind that the Fourth Princess was born in 1887, two years after the annexation in 1885, some of the accounts she recorded forty-six years later in 1931 could have been hearsay.

This I believe is the final humiliation of Burma.

CHAPTER II

THE BRITISH AND THE BURMAN COURT

The British had become aware of Burma, that mysterious kingdom of rubies and golden pagodas, soon after the visit of Ralph Fitch in 1586-7. At the time, Fitch referred to it as 'the kingdom of Bagou, corruptly called Pegu'.[1] (This was the name of the capital of the old Mon kingdom which had been annexed by the Burmans in 1539.) Fitch was the first of the English merchants whose activities were to result in the total subjugation of the country to the British Empire in 1885. These traders, with certain honourable exceptions, were grasping and rapacious, quick to rob, lie and cheat the natives. They were supposedly Christians but the only altar at which they worshipped was that of Mamon.

British trade with Burma may be said to date from 1617, when the East India Company sent Henry Forest and John Staveley to Dagon (Rangoon) to ask for the return of the property of Thomas Samuel. The latter had died in Syriam while trading on their behalf and his belongings had been seized by the authorities. Although the pair were welcomed by King Anaukpetlun (r. 1605-28) and exchanged presents, they failed to discuss the matter for which they had been sent. Finally, running out of money, they returned to the Company's headquarters at Masulipatam in India. However, they did carry a letter from the King in which he expressed 'his desire to give free trade and entertainment to the English nation, if they would with their shipping repair unto his country'.[2] It is interesting to note the manner of men sent by the Company to the ruler of a foreign country from whom they wanted favours. William Methwold, the officer in charge at Masulipatam, described them as being 'royotous, vitious and unfaithful' and of Forest he said that he was 'a vearie villane, debaucht, most audacios and dishonest'.[3]

In 1647, the Company began trading officially with Burma, using the port of Syriam (immediately south-east of Rangoon) as its base. King Thalun (r. 1629-48) later gave it permission to build a house and a dock there. At first, trade was good, making a 40 per cent profit on the first voyage, but soon, the merchants were up to their old tricks. The Burmese were anxious to buy cotton goods, but only of good quality. Instead, all they were being offered was inferior cloth that would not sell in India. This is evident from a letter from the suppliers, Messrs Greenhill and Gurney, to the Company which concluded: 'lastly be pleased to take notice that wee are advised from the Bay [of Bengal] the broadcloth sent thither proves soe damnified as it will not vend there, for which cause it is intended for Pegu'.[4]

In 1680, Sir Streynsham Master, the Agent-Governor of Fort St George, (the Company's headquarters at Madras) sent an envoy to King Minrekyawdin (r. 1673-98) seeking permission for the Company's traders to 'voyage to and fro at their pleasure in pursuance of their trade, sell, buy, and barter according to the Custome of the Country' free from any 'let or hindrance' by the King's Governors or Ministers, and to 'tarry there as long as they think good and depart the Country again when they please'.[5]

These demands must surely have been made tongue in cheek, for had the King accepted them, he would not only have given up his monopolies over such resources as rubies, timber, and oil, which all belonged to him, but also would have been unable to collect taxes on imports and exports. The next attempt fifteen years later went to the opposite extreme. Edward Fleetwood and James Lesly were furnished with a calculatingly obsequious letter from Nathaniel Higginson, the Governor of Fort St George, which began:

> To his Imperial Majesty, who blesseth the noble city of Ava, with his presence, Emperour of Emperours, and excelling the Kings of the East and West...who feareth none and is feared by all...whose bright-ness shines throughout the world,....[6]

Higginson asked the King to allow the Right Honourable Company to permit factors 'to buy and sell, in such commoditys and under such Privileges, as your Royall bounty shall please to grant'. Predictably, such a servile approach had the desired effect on the Burmese Court, which had delusions of being a leading power. Among the dispensations, the King allowed the abatement of one third of the customs duties to ships of the Company. Trade continued successfully for some time and was found to be mutually beneficial, if somewhat limited. Any small problems such as the giving of *let-saung* 'presents' to officials (palm-greasing as it might be called), were taken in their stride, the cost being 'added on'.

In 1753, the next move by the Company was to take over the strategically placed Island of Negrais (known to the Burmese as Haing-gyi-kyun), since from the island it was possible to trade throughout the kingdom, and the place could be fortified. Having first built a settlement on the island, the Company then waited two years before requesting permission from Alaungmintaya (r. 1752-60). On this occasion, it seems to have got more than it asked for as the King was in desperate need of firearms to fight the Mon of Lower Burma. His price for allowing them to stay at Negrais was one thousand muskets and twenty pieces of cannon. Further, it was also granted the right to settle at Pathein (Bassein) and at the old Mon town of Dagon (soon to be changed in 1755 to Yangon or End of Threat (from the Mon) and later anglicized to Rangoon). The King had plans to build a new town and port at Dagon after he had captured the Mon kingdom of Pegu.

All would perhaps have been well for the Company had it not been for the resident Armenian and French traders who were becoming jealous of their British counterparts. The latter had originally been made prisoners by the King when he discovered that they had been supporting his enemies the Mon. Later they had been allowed to settle in the area. They now made trouble by persuading him that the British were secretly aiding the Mon. If they were, it would not have been for the first time. Indeed, on one occasion whilst British and French ships were firing on the Burmese camp at Syriam in support of the Mon, a British mission was being received by Alaungmintaya at his capital, Shwebo in Upper Burma, to discuss a treaty of friendship and commerce.

The French in particular needed no persuasion to damage the British interest, although it must be said that the British were quite able to do this themselves. It seemed that during the war between the Burmese and the Mon, the head of the settlement at Negrais had given four or five muskets, powder, shot and and some provisions to the latter. Needless to say, these paltry amounts were not diminished in the telling, and according to Sir Arthur Phayre the report of a greater amount was probably well founded. It was further put to the King that the British would fortify the island, bring in military stores and men, and when they were strong enough take over the country, as they had done in Bengal and on the coast. There was just enough truth in the matter to cause the King, who was by now thoroughly disenchanted with the perfidious Europeans, to act. He therefore ordered that all the foreigners on Negrais be killed and the settlement burnt to the ground. And so it was done, and ten Europeans and over one hundred Indians were massacred. A few, however, escaped and some Englishmen were taken prisoner to Yangon.

From the date of the massacre on 5 October 1759, there was virtually no contact between Britain and Burma until 1795. In that year, the Governor-General of India, Sir John Shore, sent Captain Michael Symes to the Burmese Court to negotiate a commercial treaty. It included the right to appoint an agent at Rangoon, to conduct commerce, and finally to discuss the frontier between the Burmese and English territories. This last point was made necessary due to the Burmese having annexed Arakan in 1784; they were then separated from the British province of Chittagong only by the Naaf River. As expected, it was not long before serious trouble occurred, for the overbearing Burmese treated the inhabitants of Arakan harshly. The situation became so unbearable that thousands fled into Chittagong where they were allowed to settle.

Meanwhile, in Arakan three Arakanese chiefs remained and carried out a guerilla style resistance for some years, but finally they too were forced to flee into British territory. Once this became known at the Burmese capital Amarapura, a general with five thousand men was sent into Chittagong to demand their return. There he met the British General Erskine who agreed to enquire into the Burmese demands and who later handed over the three Arakanese chiefs, two of whom were promptly executed. Phayre was to comment that: 'The surrender of these patriots must be condemned as an act unworthy of a civilized power, having an armed force at command.'[7]

In 1795 the mission headed by Symes was well received at the Burmese Court despite the fact that he had been sent by the Governor-General of India and not the British King. This was a source of constant annoyance to King Badon (r. 1782-1819) and subsequent Burmese monarchs who considered themselves the most powerful of kings, and far superior to a mere governor-general who could be removed at the whim of the British parliament. To his credit, Symes achieved most of his objectives and later wrote an account of his embassy.[8] From this it can be seen that he had an open and lively mind, and was interested in all that he observed. Without condescension he recognized that the Burmese were insular and had little idea of anything happening outside their own country, and that as far as Europeans were concerned they were a backward people.

All this he accepted and framed his negotiations accordingly, and ended his mission by sending a favourable report on the Burmese to the Governor-General. Curiously, Phayre dismissed Symes embassy very briefly: 'he was received with dubious courtesy. He obtained a delusive order as to trade, but no treaty; and no reply from the King was sent to the Governor-General's letter.'[9] The fact that a reply was indeed sent by the King appeared as appendix three in Symes's account. One of Symes' instructions had been to get permission for a British Agent to be Resident at Rangoon, and in 1796, Captain Hiram Cox was appointed to this post, but he proved to be an unfortunate choice. It would appear that Cox was a man with ideas above his station, and indeed, above the terms of his appointment, feeling that he should be treated as an ambassador. Htin Aung observed that Cox was surprised, hurt and angry when he did not receive the deference to which he was not entitled. His attempts at self aggrandizement at the Burmese Court led to him being ignored, and after nine months he left in disgust and returned to Rangoon from where he was recalled. The Government of India later sent a letter of apology to the Burmese, accepting that the responsibility for the failure of the mission rested with Cox. Without doubt, Cox had fixed ideas of his own and was prejudiced towards the Burmese before he went. As a result of his humiliating experience he wrote a journal in which he described the Burmese Court as 'an assembly of clowns', and their followers as 'ungrateful, rapacious, cruel, treacherous, avaricious and lazy'. According to Woodman, the text provided Dr Bayfield with data for what she described as one of the most malicious accounts of the country.[10]

In 1797 there was further trouble on the Arakan frontier as the exodus of Arakanese into Chittagong increased. Once again the Burmese sent troops into British territory to demand their return, but after a show of force they withdrew. A Burmese agent then arrived in Calcutta and in no uncertain terms asked for the fugitives to be sent back. At the time Lord Wellesley, the newly appointed Governor-General, had more immediate concerns in India and Afghanistan and was too busy to take notice of a border dispute. Nevertheless, he replied that the immigrants would not be allowed to make raids into Arakan, although this was clearly an impossible promise to keep. The Governor of Arakan then threatened to invade Chittagong if the Arakanese were not returned.

When local negotiations failed, Symes (now Colonel) was again sent to Amarapura. He arrived in Rangoon in May 1802 with instructions from Lord Wellesley. The primary objective of the mission was to demonstrate the superiority of the British both in military and commercial terms, and to this end a large military escort accompanied him. This escort might be called upon to perform duties other than the ceremonial, since it had come to the ears of the Governor-General that the elderly King might die or abdicate whilst Symes was in the country. He was instructed that:

> His Excellency in council directs me to observe that such a state of events would precisely constitute that crisis of affairs which is most to be desired for the purpose of establishing the British influence and of promoting British interests in the Burmese Empire.[11]

In the probability of such an event taking place, Symes was to offer the British troops to the Burmese heir apparent to support the regular succession. (Had the King known of this he could hardly fail to have been amused since he had considered offering Burmese troops to Lord Wellesley to aid Britain in her war with France.) Advice to Symes continued:

> His Excellency considers it extremely desirable that the Government of Ava should consent to subsidize permanently the British force, which may be furnished on this occasion, or even a larger portion of British troops, and His Excellency accordingly desires that in the event supposed, you will exert your endeavours for the attainment of that important object.[12]

At this point the French arrived on the stage. Previously they had been in the wings, with their factories in India and occasional trading visits to Rangoon, but now there was talk of an alliance between Burma and France. Symes was required to nip this in the bud. He was told to say that

> it seems impossible that the Court of Ava could balance between the policy of connecting itself with a nation possessed of no resources on this quarter of the globe, and [or] with a power capable from its local situation and magnitude of its resources, of being either a formidable foe, or a powerful ally of the Burman Empire.[13]

Plate 2. An Attawoon or Minister of the Interior and his Wife (left), and a Seredogee or Secretary of State (right) in their dress of ceremony. From Symes' *First Embassy... 1794.*

Plate 3. A Birman Peasant and his Wife. From Symes' *First Embassy... 1794.*

Symes was to explain to the Government of Ava 'the danger to which its interests would be exposed by a connection with France'. He was told that:

His Excellency considers the exclusion of the subjects of France [from] any establishment within the Dominions of Ava, and the supersession of their influence in the concerns of that state, to be objects of the greatest importance.[14]

Symes' reception during his second visit in 1802 was markedly different from his first and he was treated with Oriental discourtesy. This is so subtle as to go unnoticed by the average Westerner, in which case much satisfaction was gained by insulting a foreigner who was too ignorant to realize what was happening. Fortunately, Symes would not rise to this bait, for he realized that most of his problems were caused by the Armenian traders who conducted much of the King's commercial business and the impending arrival of a so-called French delegation in Amarapura. This mission turned out to be a very damp squib indeed, and the King soon got rid of it and began to look more favourably on Symes who, as a result, attained most of his objectives. These included permission to have an Agent resident at Rangoon.

In 1803, Lieutenant Canning was appointed to this joyless post, and had to negotiate with the Burmese officials who were anti-British to a man. Also, as the British representative he had to police the actions of the British traders of whom Symes had written:

I wish it were in my power to report favourably of the conduct of the generality of British subjects, who reside at, and trade to this place. Their number at present amounts to about 60, some of whom (but I am sorry to add, very few) are men of respectable conduct.[15]

Regarding the French traders, Canning wrote: 'I have not been able to discover that any agent in the pay of France resides at Rangoon, the few French that are there are of the lowest and most despicable class...'[16] Canning (now promoted to Captain), had found his feet despite having a few problems, with the result that his thoughts now turned to the expansion of British territories. He wrote and suggested to the authorities in Calcutta the annexation of Arakan, since 'The possession of Arakan offers considerable advantages to the British Government to which it seems destined by nature to belong, being a continuation of the plane that extends from Chittagong as far as Cape Negrais, and bounded on the east by the high range of mountains that anciently formed the boundry of the Burmese Empire.'[17] Canning argued that if the Burmese were not overlords of Arakan, then Chittagong would not be threatened by them.

It so happened that the King of Burma's reasoning was on similar lines. He felt that were he to take Chittagong and East Bengal he would not be threatened in Arakan by the Arakanese insurgents, who were, it seemed, permitted to use British territories as a base for their incursions. Surprisingly, by the second half of the eighteenth century and after their annexation of Arakan, the Bur-

Plate 4. A Kioum or Monastery. From Symes' *First Embassy... 1794.*

Plate 5. A Birman War Boat. From Symes' *First Embassy... 1794.*

mese had laid claim to Bengal. As early as the thirteenth century Marco Polo had mistakenly described the King of Pagan as also the King of Bengala. Certainly, Phayre accepted that the Arakanese kings held Chittagong in the seventeenth century, and captured part of the Bakirgunj in Bengal. They took Dacca with the help of Portuguese mercenaries and levied tribute from it. As the present ruler of Arakan, the King of Burma felt that he had inherited a claim to those parts of British India.

The situation remained literally in a state of armed neutrality until 1811, when the Arakanese patriot, Chin Pyan, invaded Arakan. Known also as 'Kingbering' to the British, he was the son of an Arakanese chief who had earlier fled to Chittagong. Father and son had amassed a large body of their compatriots, probably about 20,000, and were determined to free their country from the Burmese yoke.[18] Armed and provisioned, Chin Pyan's army acquired boats to take it across the Naaf River and into its homeland. The King of Burma was furious that the British appeared to be aiding his subjects in their rebellion. He drew no distinction as to where they lived, for as ruler of Arakan all Arakanese owed him allegiance.

Hall echoed Phayre when he wrote: 'The Burmese Government had just cause of complaint, for the weakness or the neglect by which the refugees who enjoyed British protection were left without control.'[19] Chin Pyan overran much of Arakan and succeeded in taking the capital Mrauk U. This was without the help of the British for whose assistance he had pleaded in vain. Unfortunately his untrained men could not hold the newly won territories. As a result, when the Burmese poured in fresh troops he had no alternative but flee to the mountains. Many of his followers, however, escaped to Chittagong.

It is perhaps not too far-fetched a scenario to imagine that the Government of India, recognising Captain Canning's argument on the annexation of Arakan, thought of another way of achieving his design. Chin Pyan had appealed to the Governor-General, offering to rule Arakan under the protection of the British. The offer was refused since any open interference in Arakan would have meant war with the Burmese. Possibly it was thought that turning a blind eye in not seeing an army of 20,000 men, together with the import of 20,000 muskets and at a hundred rounds each, two million rounds of ammunition, would enable Chin Pyan to achieve his aim. And perhaps, once the Burmese had been overthrown, a protectorate might be offered. However, according to Phayre: 'By the supiness of the British Government, Chin Pyan was still allowed to raid on the frontier of Arakan.'[20] Unfortunately Chin Pyan failed to achieve his objective and instead became an embarrassment to the British. Phayre added that 'the government, with a discreditable disregard of its own character, allowed Burmese troops to enter the hills within British territory to attack the chief in his stronghold'.[21] And so the Burmese remained in control in Arakan and now looked toward the small weak states of Assam and Manipur.

Since the thirteenth century, when the Shans conquered Ahthan (Assam), Burma had seldom intefered there except when asked. The Assamese were considered by the Burmese to be Shans, and as long as they recognized the nominal supremacy of the Burmese kings, were treated as other Shans, as masters in their own states.

The British were aware of Burma's interest in Assam as early as 1797, during Captain Cox's time in Amarapura. Indeed, Phayre writes that in that year preparations were made to invade Assam but were countermanded. Harvey gives details of two incursions by the Burmese into Assam in 1805, but by means of bribes the generals were induced to withdraw.[22] In 1809 the British were asked by Assamese officials to intervene in their internal problems at court, but the request was turned down. By 1816, after the British had again refused their plea, they had no alternative but to submit a further application to the King of Burma, who late in that year sent an army to restore the ruler to his throne. After payment of a large indemnity the Burmese army withdrew in April 1817.

Two years later, they were again asked to help the ruler, Chandra Kant, who had been deposed by the simple method of slitting his ear. According to Assamese custom, being thus mutilated he was disqualified from occupying the throne. However, the Burmese, under Kyee Mingyi, disregarded this small matter, since, as he was to be their puppet, they were not concerned with the niceties of Assamese kingship.

Nevertheless, by April 1821 Chandra Kant had cause to worry about the high-handed Burmese attitude and his own safety, for he was well aware that he was only a figurehead who could be summarily replaced. He therefore thought it prudent to flee to British territory where once again the British allowed their territory to be used as a base for attacks on the Burmese. This time British support was active instead of tacit.

Regarding the kingdom of Manipura (Manipur), earlier in 1758, the son of the Raja had invited the Burmese King Alaungmintaya to come and settle the succession to the throne. Accordingly, he entered that country with a massive force, received the submission of the chiefs, and confirmed the young Prince in his position.

One of his successors, Myaidu Min (r. 1763-76), attacked Manipur in 1764 as punishment for border incursons made by the Raja, and took many of its people to increase the population of his new capital Ava. The Kubo Valley which lay between the Manipuri border and the Chindwin River was also annexed, and the Raja was duly reminded of his vassalage. The Burmese regarded this action as no more and no less than similar to the British conquests in India.

Certainly there appears to have been no recorded remonstrance by the British at the time.

There was further trouble in Manipur in 1819, when Raja Marjit Singh refused to pay his respects by attending the coronation of Sagaing Min (r. 1819-37). As far as the Burmese Court was concerned this was a treasonable offence and a strong force was immediately dispatched to depose him. Singh fled to the neighbouring state of Eggapat (Cachar), and with his brothers deposed the ruler of that country. The ousted Raja Govind Chandra promptly applied to the British for assistance and protection, but was refused. He therefore turned to the King of Burma, who sent troops to re-instate him.

By 1819 the British had decided enough was enough, as the Burmese presence was coming too close to their territories for comfort. They had tried unsuccessfully to persuade the Burmese to join with them in determining the frontier between their two spheres of interest, but the King of Burma admitted to no boundaries. Instead, the Governor of Arakan, speaking with authority it seems, declared that if the King were thwarted, he would take by force the cities of Dacca and Murshidabad and invade Bengal and Chittagong. As a result, an about turn in policy was ordered, where previously the rulers of Assam and Cachar had been refused assistance, it was now imposed upon them, as was the case with the ruler of the tiny hill state of Waythali (Jaintia).

Honesty, however, demands that the untiring efforts of the British to prevent war should be recorded, and that the Burmese provoked the conflict. Whether this was through ignorance or arrogance cannot now be known, although judging by Burmese sources, one has the feeling that it was both. The inflated Burman notions of their power were such that they genuinely believed they had a divine right to which ever country they invaded. Their rulers delighted in grandiose titles such as King of Kings and expected other rulers to bow submissively to them. The state propaganda machine was one of the finest in the world, and ceaselessly indoctrinated the already timid and downtrodden inhabitants with claims that their king had in his possession fairy spears and supernatural swords which could conquer all enemies. Surrounding kingdoms were seen as vassal states from which virgin daughters and tribute could be demanded at will. In fact, as far as the king was concerned, all his subjects were regarded as *nga-kyun* (my slaves). This curious state of affairs survives today in the word *kyun-daw* (your royal slave) which Burman males use when either writing or addressing their equals or superiors.

From the second half of the 1700s the Burmese possibly took their lead from the British who had, from their humble trading posts, made themselves undisputed masters of India. But little did they know that by the early 1820s they were playing a dangerous game. Suffice it to say that on 5 March 1824, Lord Amherst, the Governor-General of India, declared war on the Empire of Burma.

Plate 6. The Royal Palace at Ava (Inn Wa) in the 1820s.

Chapter III

The First Anglo-Burmese War, 1824-6

The first Anglo-Burmese war of 1824-6 proved a disaster for both protagonists. By the time it concluded with the treaty of Yandabo, signed on 24 February 1826 by General Sir Archibald Campbell and the Ministers of the Burmese Court, it had cost Britain £15,000,000 and the lives of 15,000 British and Indian troops, although £1,000,000 was later recovered from the Burmese in indemnity. This figure of fifteen million was later to be questioned by Lord Dalhousie early in the second war. Writing to a friend on 10 July 1852, he commented that he did not believe the first war had cost that sum, and that the only way such a figure could be arrived at was if the entire pay of the troops was taken into account, rather than just the extra costs of the war. He had, he said, from the official records a figure of £150,000 expenditure during the most costly period. This, if multiplied by the twenty-four months of the campaign, would only produce a cost of £3,600,000.

According to Hall it was 'the worst-managed war in British military history', for the lack of military planning was apparent from the outset.[1] Trusting to favourable reports by their intelligence agents, the British felt so confident that they would be treated as liberators by the long suffering inhabitants on their arrival in Rangoon, that they took only sufficient provisions for a few days. However, when they entered the town on 11 May 1824, they found it deserted, a strategy which was organized by the Burmese authorities. Major Snodgrass, General Campbell's Military Secretary wrote:

> Deserted, as we found ourselves, by the people of the country, from whom we alone could expect supplies - unprovided with the means of moving either by land or water, and the rainy season just setting in - no prospect remained to us but that of a long residence in the miserable and dirty hovels of Rangoon, trusting to the transports [from Calcutta] for provisions with such partial supplies as our foraging parties might procure... by distant and fatiguing marches into the interior of the country.[2]

Regarding this appalling turn of events, two questions immediately arise. Why did the British begin their campaign at the start of the rainy season which lasted for four long months? This meant that they would be tied down, as nothing could move because of the rain storms. And why was their intelligence so deficient concerning the expected response from the people of the country? The answers can only be guessed at but are a sad reflection on the cabilities of the British commanders.

By the end of July 1824 Rangoon was one vast field hospital, with the troops suffering from gastro-intestinal diseases due to bad sanitation and a lack of clean water. Other problems were malaria (although not recognized as such at the time) and scurvy due to the non existance of fresh produce. Eventually, local European traders began chartering vessels to bring in supplies which they then sold at a vast profit to those who were able to pay. One entrepreneur even went so far as to buy all the beer from the rather naïve master of a ship in the Rangoon river, and promptly made a profit of 10,000 rupees on the deal.

News about the sorrowful plight of the British army spread along the coastal ports, and once the monsoon was over enterprising Chinese purveyors from Penang began arriving with fresh provisions. It may be imagined how lucrative this trade turned out to be. Another question which remains to be asked, is why did the Burmese not attack this weakened force which had invaded their kingdom? The answer lies in the fact that it was a tradition among the Burmese not to go to war during the monsoon season as they were only too aware of the difficulties involved in the movement of troops and animals.

By December 1824, despite the improved supplies, nearly half the European troops who had landed in May had died. Of the conduct of the war, it can only be said that it was typical of its time and the lives of men were wasted by over-enthusiastic officers attempting to achieve instant success. In battle, the British army was conspicuous beyond belief. Its men, dressed in bright red serge uniforms, invariably marched in the sweltering heat to the sounds of a noisy band and without due regard for the snipers concealed within the surrounding jungle.

The superstitious Burmese were at first awed and believed that, to flaunt themselves so bravely, either these white warriors were bullet-proof or else carried powerful talismans. But soon awe turned to derision. The British had only to see a stockade to attack it; despite its construction of either huge teak logs or palm tree trunks, strengthened behind with earthworks. On one occasion, a determined but pointless assault was only called off because there were no more unwounded British officers to lead it.

As was the custom at the time, British officers always led from the front. Although this showed great bravery and inspired it in their troops, it was not a good use of manpower and was responsible for many an untimely death. On the other hand, Burmese officers tended to direct from the rear. It was said that Shan and other ethnic conscripts who were considered expendable, were made to march in the vanguard, thus being the first to meet with enemy fire. The Burman soldiers then took evasive action.

Although brave, as admitted by individual British officers, the Burmans were in the main an army of conscripted civilians. Nevertheless, there was a small standing army, largely ceremonial, at the capital. Ranged against this ragtag and bobtail force, which was armed with spears, bows and arrows and ancient muskets, were ranged disciplined European soldiers and native sepoys with superior weapons. The result was inevitable. That the fighting in Lower Burma took two years to resolve highlights the difficulties faced by the British commander mainly with the weather, sickness, provisions and transport.

However, General Campbell did have good luck on his side, since the battle plan of the Burmese Commander-in-Chief Maha Bandula was fatally flawed. Bandula placed his men in stockades, thus concentrating them in a small area from which they fired into the British who attempted to storm them. He also relied on the sheer volume of numbers to achieve his aims. This had worked before, but only against other Oriental armies. The British, however, quickly found that only the strongest stockade could withstand their heavy cannon. And the effect of an exploding shell within the confines of a fortification can scarcely be imagined.

When Bandula attacked the British on 1 December 1824 next to the Shwe Dagon pagoda, Rangoon's premier Buddhist shrine, he had 30,000 men, only half of whom were armed with muskets. Htin Aung records that by the end of the action on the ninth, Bandula had lost 13,000 men.[3] The British had 10,000 men in the field, and according to Bruce their losses were 30 killed and 220 wounded.[4]

There is a considerable discrepancy concerning the number of troops in this engagement. While Htin Aung quotes 30,000 Burmese troops and 10,000 British, he puts the loss to the Burmese at 13,000. On the other hand, Phayre states that the figure for the Burmese was 60,000.[5] Like Phayre, Bruce also quotes 60,000 men which included 35,000 musketeers, several hundred light gunners and 700 cavalry. Hall also has 60,000 Burmese with a considerable artillery train, but reduces the British force to 4,000. Pearn, who quoted from General Campbell's report, wrote that there were 50,000 Burmese present. However, it was not unknown for Campbell to exaggerate the strength of his enemy – implying that the British needed only a few to vanquish a vast horde sent against them.[6] Finally, the official Burmese record in the form of the *Konbaungset Yazawin* (Konbaungset Chronicle) gives the more likely figure of 16,000 men in the royal army.[7]

In these encounters, had Bandula used his men as guerillas to starve and harass the sick and enfeebled British rather than to stage a set piece battle, the outcome of the war might have been quite different. Such tactics were subsequently used successfully against the British in Afghanistan.

After the defeat at Rangoon, Bandula withdrew his troops to the strongly fortified town of Danubyu on the Irrawaddy, some seventy-five kilometres to the north-west and awaited the arrival of the British. He knew that if he controlled the river he could prevent or at least delay their advance on the royal capital, which had now been transferred back to the old city site of Ava. The British had divided their forces into a river and a land column, the latter relying

The storming of the Kemmendine stockade on the 10 June 1824.

Plates 7 and 8.

British soldiers preparing to bombard a Burman stockade (1824).

The great fire of Dalla, on the Rangoon River (1824).

Plates 9 and 10.

Madras troops who fought the Burmans (1824).

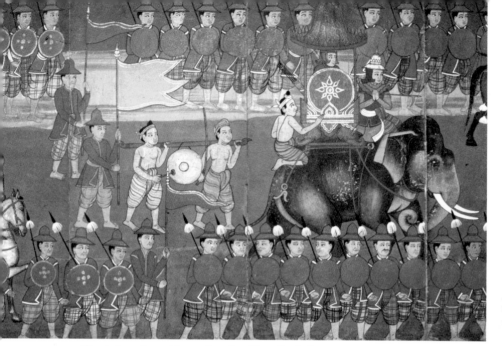

War elephant, foot soldiers and cavalry officers. Parabaik painting, *circa* 1820s.

Plates 11 and 12.

Swordsmen and gunners. Parabaik painting, *circa* 1820s.

Plate 13. Burman hlaw-gar (warboats). Parabaik painting based on a 19th century manuscript.

View of the Landing at Rangoon of Part of the Combined Forces from Bengal and Madras, under the Orders of Sir Archibald Campbell, K.C.B. on 11 May 1824.

Plates 14 and 15.

The Attack on the Stockades at Pagoda Point, on the Rangoon River, by Sir Archibald Campbell, KCB. 8 July 1824.

The Principal approach to the Great Dagon Pagoda at Rangoon (1824).

Plates 16 and 17.

View of the Great Dagon Pagoda and adjacent scenery on the Eastern Road from Rangoon (1824).

View of the Great Dagon Pagoda at Rangoon and scenery adjacent to the Westward of the Great Road (1824).

Plates 18 and 19.

View of the Lake and part of the Eastern Road from Rangoon, taken from advance of the 7th Madras Native Infantry (1824).

Plate 20. Scene Upon the Terrace of the Great Dagon Pagoda at Rangoon, taken near the Great Bell (1824).

Plate 21. Bandula's look-out tree at Danbuyu – mounting four guns.

on the former for supplies, troops, medical care etc., but when the flotilla of vessels failed to get past the stockade at Danubyu, the advance was halted. To attack Bandula, General Campbell, who was leading the land column, had to return and combine with General Cotton, who was in charge of the water column.

During this encounter, on 1 April 1825 Bandula was killed by a chance shell from a mortar tube. This was to all intents and purposes the end of the Burmese resistance. On the death of their general, the army realized the impossibility of winning a war in which all the odds were against it. From now on it adopted a rearguard action, a mere delay of the inevitable as it fled back towards Ava. Sporadic actions took place as Campbell persued his inexorable journey up the Irrawaddy towards the capital, but these did not persist, for want of imaginative Burmese generals to rally their forces. Finally, at Yandabo, only three days march from Ava, the King accepted Campbell's terms.

The Burmese were humiliated by the treaty they were forced to sign. They had to accept not only the presence of a Resident at Ava, but also the loss of Arakan, Assam and Tenasserim. Further, they were forbidden to interfere in the states of Manipur, Cachar and Jaintia. The kingdom was almost brought to bankruptcy in finding the money for the £1,000,000 indemnity which was also demanded. This was to be paid in four instalments. After the first, the British would return to Rangoon, and after the second, would leave the country. In the Delta regions neither Burman nor Mon were pleased to see the British go, for during their stay there had been law and order and freedom from the demands of rapacious native officials and their arrogant minions.

On 1 February 1825, General Campbell, the Commander of the British forces had issued a proclamation addressed to the 'Inhabitants of the Burman Empire' in which he gave the reasons for the war, and instructions to the people for their future conduct.[8] He assured them of his protection should they remain peaceful. This was a repeat of the assurance that he had given in 1824. At that time, he had urged the people (who were predominantly Mon) to place themselves under the protection of the British flag. The Mon, since the extermination of their kingdom by King Alaungmintaya in 1757, considered themselves under the thrall of the Burmese and thus saw the proclamation as a guarantee of the restoration of their independence under British protection. Pearn wrote:

> It was true that the Treaty of Yandabo provided for a general amnesty for all who had taken part in the war, but such provision was not likely to be regarded once the garrison had left, and there was a good deal of feeling among both Mon and English that the Government of India, in concluding the treaty of Yandabo which placed the Mon at the mercy of those against whom they had fought, had been guilty of a act of betrayal, especially as protection had been explicitly promised them.[9]

Many of the Mon left the areas under Burmese rule and settled in British Tenasserim or Arakan, while others stayed behind and raised the standard of rebellion. Lamentably, this was short lived and bloody as the Burmese were determined to crush them once and for all. When the Mon were finally defeated, about ten thousand fled to Tenasserim where their leader, Maung Sat was given a pension by the British.

It might almost be thought that even before the first war was won, the second was being planned by the British. As soon as Rungpur, the capital of Assam was reached by Captain Neufville, a British officer, in 1825, he was exploring the route to Burma through the Hukawng Valley. Unfortunately, this survey was hampered by the local war-like Kachins who, while no friends of their Burmese overlords, had no desire to see their ancestral lands fall to the British.

The An Pass between Arakan and Burma, too, was being explored by a Captain Ross in 1826 to determine its potential use by British troops. As he remarked at the time, 'in any future war with the Burmese this knowledge may be of great importance, leading as the route does into the very heart of the Burmese Empire'.[10]

In September 1826, the Governor-General of India sent John Crawfurd to Ava to discuss the signing of a commercial treaty. It is interesting to note that Woodman scarcely notices this in her book *The Making of Burma*.[11] In his *The*

Plate 22. Meeting of the British and Burmese commissioners. Principal figure, the Kee-wongee.

Stricken Peacock, Htin Aung described Crawfurd as being 'unbending, aloof' and with a 'contemptuous attitude to the Burmese'.[12] He was no less scathing in his *A History of Burma* where he says that 'Crawfurd must be given the credit as the innovator of the campaign of defamation and calumny against the Burmese, which, continued by others, led to the Second Anglo-Burmese war'. Hall, too, paints a picture of a man quite out of his depth.

Crawfurd came with a draft of twenty-two articles but was out-manoeuvred by the Burmese negotiators who agreed to only four. But of these four, two were to become pivotal in British Burmese relations. They included: 'mutual freedom of trade for British merchants in Burma and Burmese merchants in India' and 'freedom of movement for merchants in the two countries'.[13] Yule noted that after the negotiations, Crawfurd was 'rendered weary, hopeless and disgusted by the arrogance and impracticability of the Burmese Ministers'.[14]

It would seem that on this occasion the Burmese had got the upper hand, but quite the contrary. Crawfurd was more successful than he realized. The previously closed kingdom was now wide open and any Englishman – soldier, spy, trader or missionary – could wander the country at will.

Major Henry Burney, who had been appointed Resident at the Court of Ava in 1830, was particularly interested in the Hukawng Valley route which gave access to the amber, jade and ruby mines, and to Bhamo and China. Nevertheless, it was not until 1835 that he saw a chance of obtaining more information regarding this area. As a new Burmese Governor was being sent to Mogaung, Burney managed to persuade the King to allow Captain Hannay to accompany him; this was despite the suspicions of the court officials. Nowadays, such a mission might be called commercial espionage. Hannay was instructed that:

> It would be useful for you to ascertain as many routes as you can from Bhamo into China, and from Mogaung into Assam. You will also take particular pains to ascertain how far the plan proposed by Captain Jenkins of establishing a regular route between Suddiya [in eastern Assam] and the Burmese dominions is likely to succeed.... taking every opportunity of pointing out to the Governor of Mogaung and other Burmese officials the great advantage and convenience to themselves of establishing a regular trade route between their country and Suddiya.[15]

Burney must have realized that he was going against the wishes of the King, since had he desired this trade he would have ordered it by this very same route. During the journey, Hannay sent a sepoy with Burmese guides to find the road from Maingkom, the capital of the Hukawng Valley, to Assam, which he duly did. Burney, when informed of this, wrote to the Government of India suggesting:

> that some pretext should be found for sending an officer from Assam to me here via Maingkom and Mogaung. After two or three such occasions not only a trade between Assam and this country [Burma] would be placed on a more secure footing, and I think the Court of Ava would remove the prohibition which it now imposes on our traders proceeding above Ava towards Bhamo and Mogaung and disturbing the monopoly which the Chinese have long enjoyed of the whole trade in that quarter.[16]

However, before this, and soon after Burney had taken up his duties at the Burmese Court, he had agreed with the King that a mission be sent to the new Governor-General Lord William Bentinck at Calcutta. The aim was to try to obtain certain concessions and revisions of the Treaty of Yandabo. Burney arranged for his younger brother Captain George Burney to accompany this mission with the idea of keeping him well informed. In addition, he persuaded the envoy and his entourage to travel overland from Prome into Arakan and thence to Calcutta. This would have provided invaluable information for using this route for trade and military purposes.

Meanwhile, Burney had covertly advised his Government that the envoys should be kept waiting for an audience, which childishly it did for nearly two years. However, despite this long wait the Burmese envoys achieved one of their aims, namely the return of the Kubo Valley. This was secured with the help of Burney, who had advised the authorities that this area did not provide a defence for Manipur. And so it was arbitrarily removed from that State and returned to

Burma. This, of course, enhanced Burney's reputation at the Burmese Court.

Enjoying the favour of the Burmese administration meant that Burney was able to organize missions to visit various parts of the kingdom, in accordance with the Commercial Treaty. These were designed to encourage trade to the markets of Moulmein and Rangoon. The missions concentrated on areas of the Shan States which were closest to China and Laos, and which had their own rulers called Sawpha (Sawbwa) many of whom were antagonistic to Burma, though not openly so. They welcomed the presence of the British who they hoped would enable them to achieve independence from Burmese tyranny. This was a vain hope that the British, in the cause of commerce, did nothing to dispel.

In March 1837 Lieutenant McLeod, on a visit to Kiang Tung (Jeng Tung or Keng Tung), the capital of the Khun people in the Shan States, wrote:

> Some of the [European] traders I left here have been quarrelling amongst themselves, and I fear, giving the [Shan] officers no very good opinion of their respectability... it is a great pity that the more respectable persons do not come to Zimme [Chaing Mai in the Siamese Shan States] and this place; and the men who now carry on trade are, generally speaking, a vile set, and a disgrace to the British name.[17]

At the Burmese capital, the King had been suffering from fits of depression and insanity ever since losing the war, with the result that he had become completely dominated by his principal Queen, Ma Nu, her scheming brother the Salin Kodaw or Minthagyi, and their clique. By 1837 these two were ruling the country through fear and intimidation. Rumours began to circulate that the Queen's brother intended to usurp the throne, but in order to effect this aim, the Setkya Kodaw (the King's only son) and the Prince of Tharrawaddy (the King's full brother) had to be neutralized. On hearing of these plans, Tharrawaddy and his followers escaped to Shwebo where he raised a successful rebellion.

Throughout this tense situation, Burney, though in poor health, tried his best to act as a mediator between the two royal brothers but with little success. Tharrawaddy's personality had changed dramatically for the worse, and he vowed to destroy the power of the Queen and her brother. Burney managed to obtain an undertaking from Tharrawaddy that in return for there being no bloodshed, the King would abdicate in his favour, and that the capital would be surrendered to him. But despite giving his word, Tharrawaddy reneged on his assurance and imprisoned and tortured his adversaries and their followers and finally put them to death with the most barbarous cruelty. Also included in this general massacre was his harmless and exceedingly timid young nephew, the Setkya Kodaw, who had no pretensions to the throne.

Shortly after Tharrawaddy's accession, Burney found himself in difficulties with him over the Treaty of Yandabo and the Commercial Treaty, and observed that

> the truth is, His Majesty's military advisors are not yet prepared to quarrel with us. The Treaties which we forced upon the Burmese are

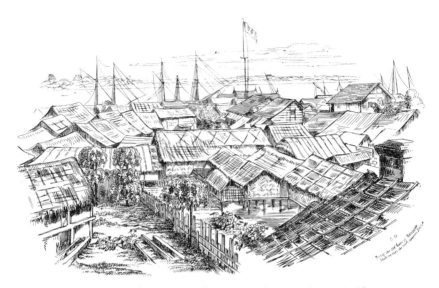

Plate 23. Part of the old town of Rangoon, looking over the river (1846).

no doubt viewed by the present as well as the late Government with much vexation and mortification...[18]

Tharrawaddy refused to recognize the treaties, saying that it was a Burmese tradition that business transacted by a previous monarch was not valid under a new administration. Such protocol was indeed rigorously upheld, for at the accession of a new king all title holders of the previous reign, be they queens, princes, ministers and the numerous grades of officials had to return their title patents and official insignia. They were then either reinstated or their status withdrawn; bribery, of course, ensured that many kept their privileges.

Tharrawaddy's attitude left Burney no alternative but to leave the capital, which he did on 17 June 1837. The King then decided arbitrarily to transfer the seat of government back to the former site of Amarapura. On arrival in Rangoon, Burney sailed for Calcutta where he gave his recommendations to the Government of India. He suggested:

> One is to leave [the king] alone for a time, and see if he will recover his reason and good sense...The other plan is, to decide at once to declare hostilities against his Majesty and frighten or beat him into reason.[19]

By then Burney had the bit between his teeth and continued to advocate war. The merchants in Rangoon, of course, were in wholehearted agreement, including the Rev. Dr Judson, the American missionary who had been imprisoned during the previous reign. Judson 'avowed himself predisposed to war, as the best, if not the only means of eventually introducing the humanising influences of the Christian religion'.[20]

Plate 24. View from the verandah of Captn Brown's residence, Rangoon (1846).

It would seem that because of his persistance, Burney was eventually rebuked by the Governor-General and his Council members, who were totally against war with Burma. Although, it must be said that at the time the British were fully committed in Afghanistan and a second war was the last thing they wanted.

Meanwhile, in Burma, Tharrawaddy was desperate for weapons, as there was unrest in various parts of his kingdom, for the Mon, Shan and Karen were plotting against him. It was no coincidence that the British had been on com-

Plate 25. Part of Rangoon from the river, at high water (1846).

mercial missions in the areas occupied by these communities. In an about face, the European merchants of Rangoon had no scruples in selling much needed arms to Tharrawaddy at an exorbitant price. They then maliciously informed the Resident that the King was buying arms to make war on the British.

In 1837, Dr Bayfield was sent to Rangoon as temporary Resident, and one of his duties was to negotiate with the Burmese Governor of the port in the disputes between that officer and the British merchants. The reputation of these traders appeared to be no different from those described earlier by General Campbell in 1828:

> Rangoon has long been notorious as an asylum for fraudulent debtors and violent and unprincipled characters from every part of India, and the only way of keeping this description of person in order and pre-venting them from disgracing the British character, imparing British interests, and disturbing the good understanding which now subsists between the British and Burmese Governments, would be by the Su-preme Government maintaining always a British officer at that port, and conferring on him the same judicial powers as are entrusted to British consuls at Constantinople and in the Barbary States.[21]

It was Bayfield's misfortune to draw the short straw, for it had been proposed that one of the merchants be appointed to this post on a monthly salary. But it was also pointed out to the Government that since they were all smuggling gold in defiance of the King's order, no one could afford to be honest enough to forgo this trade and therefore would not command the respect of his fellow traders.

Following Burney's withdrawal from the Burmese capital to Calcutta in 1837, Colonel Benson had been appointed Resident. He was succeeded by Captain McLeod, but neither felt it worthwhile staying since Tharrawaddy refused to recognize their official position. McLeod left Burma on 7 January 1840, and from then until 1851, there was no official communication with the Burmese Government.

The merchants of Rangoon began to be concerned at the lack of consular representation, where previously many of them had chafed at the supervision to which they were subjected by these officials. The feeling of the Government of India was that traders who visited unfriendly countries did so at their own risk, and should not look to their government to come to their aid in time of trouble. This view was to be completely reversed only eleven years later in 1851 and was to lead to the Second Anglo-Burmese War of 1852.

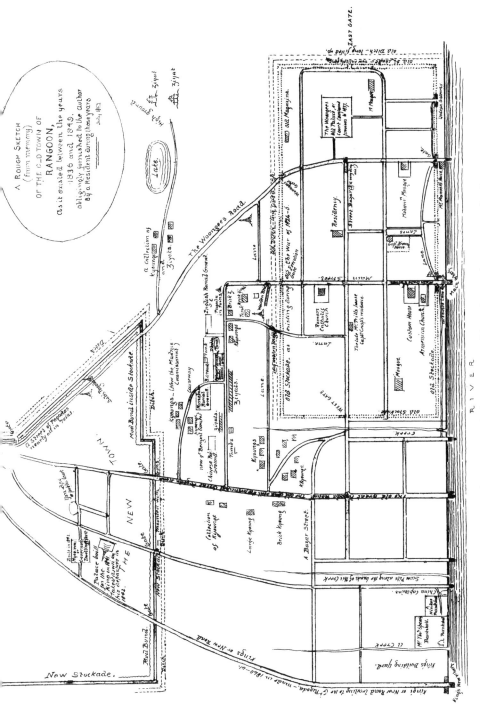

Plate 26. A rough sketch (from memory) of the old town of Rangoon, 1836-1849.

CHAPTER IV

THE SECOND ANGLO-BURMESE WAR, 1852

economics

It can be said without doubt that the second Anglo-Burmese war was provoked by the British with the active encouragement of the European merchants of Rangoon. Two primary reasons are believed to have brought about this state of affairs. The first was that the foreign traders and ships' captains who used the port of Rangoon were failing to adhere to the Burmese regulations, however harsh and arbitrary they may have appeared to be. The second involved the levying of extra taxes on foreign shipping by the Governor of Hanthawaddy (Pegu), in whose authority Rangoon fell.

In the past it was the standard practice between the British and the indigenous peoples at ports in the East for a little 'present' to oil the wheels of commerce before every transaction, but now many of these foreign traders objected to this system and were reluctant to pay. This petty display of parsimony was seen by the Burmese officials as little less than an insult. It had always been done, never spoken of, and a hint was usually sufficient. But now that it was out in the open the traders found that they had made life very difficult for themselves.

Since Rangoon was an independent Burmese port, those not wishing to submit to the notorious bureaucracy had no need to travel there. On the other hand, many did, as the rewards could be extremely lucrative. As early as AD 902, the traveller Ibn-al-Fakih reported that the area was popular with foreign merchants who came from far and wide. At the time, despite the region being in the grip of a prolonged plague epidemic, 'they flocked there, by reason of the great profits to be made'.[1]

The intention of the governor of Pegu was to levy extra taxes on those using the port and to regulate it to his and the king's advantage. As no government official in Burma was paid a salary, he took a percentage of the taxes. The richer his province the greater his reward, and with it the opportunity to purchase an even more lucrative appointment.

One such bureaucrat was Maung Ok who became Governor in 1846. It was not until 1851, however, that the British merchants began to complain of his extortions. It seemed that the Governor had overstepped the mark by arresting two ships' captains and charging them with murder and other offences. All these trumped-up charges could, of course, have been settled on the payment of a fine; indeed, had the usual 'present' been sent to the Governor and the other officials, no such charges would have been preferred. The fines were subsequently but reluctantly paid and the captains released, but they then promptly appealed to the Government of India for the reimbursement of the sums involved, totalling £1,920. However, the authorities in Calcutta saw that the captains were attempting to profit from their misfortune and reduced the sum to £920. It was on account of this sum that Pagan Min (r. 1846-53) lost half his kingdom. The King, who had been raised to the throne by the Taung Nanmadaw (Chief Queen), his scheming mother, was totally unsuitable for this role as it was widely known that as a child his mind had been enfeebled by a virulent attack of smallpox. Burmese sources claim that her nickname for him was *kyauk-yu* (unhinged-by-the-smallpox).[2] Pagan Min was a mild mannered man and the supposed cruelties attributed to him by some recent non-Burmese authors are not true. They are simply a confusion on their part with his father, Tharrawaddy.

Because of the outcry from the Rangoon merchants, Lord Dalhousie, the Governor-General of India, dispatched Commodore Lambert in November 1851 with a formal letter to demand reparation from the Governor of Pegu. In this he was acting within the guidelines set out by Lord Palmerston, the Foreign Secretary. In the Don Pacifico Affair, a Portuguese Jew had claimed British citizenship, having been born in Gibraltar. When his house in Athens was burnt down in an anti-semitic attack, he demanded compensation from the Greek Government and Palmerston ensured that he got it by sending a naval squadron to blockade the Greek coast. When Palmerston was censured by the Lords on 29 June 1850, he justified his action to the Commons by making a comparison between the British and Roman Empires. He said that just as a Roman could claim his rights anywhere in the world with the words *civis Romanus sum* (I am a Roman citizen),

> so also a British subject in whatever land he may be shall feel confident that the watchful eye and the strong arm of England will protect him against injustice and wrong.[3]

Unfortunately, the selection by Dalhousie of Lambert for this important role was an unwise one, for he proved to be an utterly incapable negotiator. His instructions were that should the Governor refuse to return the fines, he was to send the letter to the King in Amarapura, about four hundred miles (640 km) away. On arrival in Rangoon however, and without giving that official the opportunity to act, Lambert insisted that the letter be dispatched. He made no effort to ascertain the veracity of the claims put to him by the Rangoon merchants, who were all now attempting to get on the bandwagon. In a Minute from the Blue Book (the general name given to the reports and documents printed by the British Parliament, so called because they were generally bound with blue paper) which was censored at the time, the Governor-General wrote:

> The long list of injuries given unto Commodore Lambert, and other cases since laid before the Government of India, ought not to be en-

tertained. Many of them are of old date, none are accompanied with proof, none were preferred at the time, nor, until the appearance of the squadron off Rangoon suggested an opportunity for deriving some profit from the occasion.[4]

Lord Dalhousie's letter to the King required that the Governor be removed and a new one appointed with powers to settle the demands of the British. Surprisingly, the King readily agreed to this. Even more surprisingly, edicts and royal orders which have survived indicate that the Court had been preparing for the worst. In an edict issued as early as March 1851, the King had ordered his standing army to prepare for war, so that when the time came it could 'go down to Hanthawaddy and destroy the heretic *thu-pon, kula, Aein-ga-leik* (the rebel English)'.[5] The King's reply to Dalhousie said:

> A suitable Governor shall be appointed to administer the affairs of Rangoon; and with regard to the merchants who have been unjustifiably insulted and ill treated, proper and strict enquiries shall be instituted, and in accordance with custom it shall be decided.[6]

Now, at this point one has to wonder if Lambert was not working to a secret agenda, since it is hard to believe that subsequent events were brought about by mere arrogance and stupidity. On 4 January 1852 U Hmone, the new Governor, duly arrived and the very next day Lambert sent his assistant interpreter Edwards to ask for an interview, which was immediately granted. The new Governor at once consented to remove the embargo imposed by his predecessor by which people had been prevented from communicating with the ships of Lambert's squadron (but this can scarcely have been enforced judging by the number of complainants who managed to register their claims for redress).

Later that morning, Edwards, accompanied by two captains and two officers of the steamer HMS Hermes, went to the Governor's residence to deliver Lambert's demands. On arrival, Edwards went ahead, and according to Captain Latter the following incident occurred:

> At the foot of the steps [to the residence] one of the Governor's suite drew his dagger on him, and threateningly asked him how he dared thus to approach the Governor's house. Edwards replied that he had no intention of entering without the Governor's permission. On being called into the Governor's presence, he stated that his life had been threatened, and mentioned what had occurred. The Governor sent for the offender, and punished him in the presence of Mr Edwards in the usual Burmese manner, namely, by having him taken by the hair of the head, swung round three times, his face dashed to the ground [then] dragged out by the hair and pitched down the stairs.[7]

What Edwards did not say was that he had entered the Governor's courtyard on horseback. This he would have known was quite improper. According to the Blue Book, Edwards was selected for this duty on account of his knowledge of the Burmese language, and of the manners and customs of the Burmese people

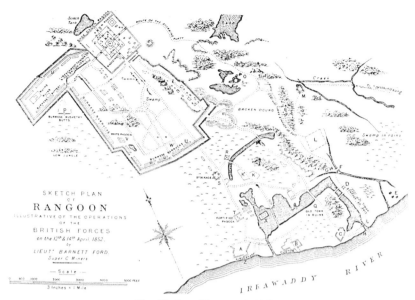

Plate 27. Plan of Rangoon in 1852.

acquired during his employment under the former Residents of the Court of Ava. Possibly he was taking his lead from Lambert who obviously held the Governor in contempt. Edwards then informed the Governor that a deputation of officers was ready to see him. They, too, arrived on horseback, having been assured by Captain Latter that any attempt to get them to dismount outside the courtyard would be a deliberate insult. Lambert no doubt knew that the strict protocol of the realm would have prevented the Governor from receiving junior officers officially; whereas, Edwards, a petty official, could be seen at any time without loss of face.

Lord Dalhousie, in his Minute, which was not printed in the Blue Book wrote:

> ...I am bound to add that in my opinion, Commodore Lambert erred in the mode in which he made his communication to the Burmese Governor, according to the known customs of that State, any communication with the chief authority of the Court of Ava should have been by means of an equal authority on the part of the British Government, the Commodore had a right to require that he should himself be received by the Burmese Governor but I apprehend he had no right to require that his inferior officers bearing his letter should be received by the Chief Governor in person.[8]

It seemed that the Governor tried to defuse the tense situation by suggesting through Edwards that Commander Fishbourne, the senior officer, be received by the Deputy Governor. The Commander, however, was not prepared to do this and so was able to report to Lambert that he and his fellow officers had been treated with disrespect by the Governor. Without waiting for any explanation from the Governor, Lambert then seized the opportunity to provoke hostilities between the two countries.

Contacting neither the Governor-General or the King in Amarapura, he gave instructions that afternoon that all British residents were to leave Rangoon on board British vessels in the harbour and were to sail that evening. The result was pandemonium. Some of the non-European merchants resident in Rangoon presented a petition to the Commodore in which, along with their prayers to him to save them from 'ruin and destruction', they said that the Governor agreed to all the demands of the British.[9] But Lambert made no reply. And as if to make doubly sure that there could be no turning back, as soon as it was dark Lambert gave orders that the King's ship *Yenanyin* (water-palace-vessel) which was moored close by the squadron, should be seized. He further, and this within ten hours of the deputation's visit to the Governor, declared that:

> In virtue of the authority from the Governor-General of British India,
> I do hereby declare the rivers of Rangoon, the Bassein and the Salween
> above Moulmein, to be in a state of blockade.[10]

Lambert then wrote to the Ministers at Amarapura informing them of his deep regret that the insults offered to him by the Governor of Rangoon had caused him to suspend further communication with the Burmese Empire. Its coasts were now blockaded, and the King's ship taken as surety for the claims for compensation made against the state.

The next morning, Lambert had the King's vessel towed to the small port of Dalla, where the Governor of that place attempted to mediate on behalf of his colleague at Rangoon. In reply, Lambert said that he would see the Governor of Rangoon if he were to come to the Commodore's flag ship and apologize for the insult to the British flag by refusing to meet the deputation sent earlier. He knew full well that the Governor could not accede to this extraordinary demand.

Lambert then received a letter from the Governor of Rangoon to say that earlier, protocol had prevented him from seeing a deputation of inferior officers, but now he was inviting Lambert to come to his residence and discuss matters. He stressed that this was the correct procedure. But Lambert was having none of this, as possibly it did not suit his purpose. He replied that the Governor had until noon the next day to comply with his demand.

At sunset the Governor sent a message to say that if the Commodore attempted to take the King's ship out of the river he would fire on him. This threat was obviously made in desparation, since the King would have had his head were he to allow the ship to be taken without any resistance. According to Lt William Laurie:

> The Commodore replied that if even a pistol were fired, he would level the stockades [which lined the river] with the ground, and with this mutual determination may be said to have commenced the second Burmese war.[11]

At daybreak on 10 January 1852 the Commodore weighed anchor and with the squadron and the merchantmen in the harbour began to escort *HMS Hermes*, which was towing the King's ship. Predictably, when they reached the stockade they were fired on. This fire was promptly returned, killing about three hundred and injuring a similar number.[12] Later that day Lambert wrote to Mr Halliday, Secretary to the Government of India:

> It is with deep regret I have had to commence hostilities with the Burmese Nation, but I am confident that the Marquis of Dalhousie and the Government of India will see it was unavoidable, and necessary to vindicate the honour of the British flag.[13]

Even then war was avoidable had Lambert wished it. To the uncharitable and deeply cynical mind it must appear that the Commodore did everything that he could to bring about the war. Conversely, he did as little as he could to prevent it. Why?

It is possible to suppose, as previously conjectured, that he was acting to a secret agenda. If so, was it his own or did it involve Lord Dalhousie? Were there

Plate 28. *Yenanyin*, the Burmese King's man-of-war, captured by the *Hermes*.

verbal instructions as well as written ones? If we look at the actions of Lord Dalhousie in the matter, at a cursory glance he seems not to have been in favour of a war with the Burmese. In his written instructions to Lambert he wrote:

> It is to be distinctly understood that no act of hostility is to be committed at present, though the reply of the Governor should be unfavourable, nor until definite instructions regarding such hostilities shall be given by the Government of India.[14]

However, he failed to remove Lambert when he first disobeyed his instructions by sending his letter to the King at Amarapura without being satisfied as to the integrity of the deponents who were claiming redress. Indeed, he went further and in a minute of the 12 January 1852, believed that the Government of India should express their 'lively satisfaction' on the way Commodore Lambert had handled the situation which had terminated in the reply of the King.

Lord Dalhousie failed to remove Lambert, even after he had committed an act of piracy by seizing the ship of the King of a country with whom Britain was not at war. And of subsequently undertaking hostilities in persuance of that act, as he wrote in the expurgated version of the Blue Book:

> I have received with much concern the intelligence conveyed in these despatches. I have perused them with the more regret that I cannot altogether exempt Commodore Lambert from the responsibility for the failure of the negotiations; and must regard him as wholly responsible for the acts of hostility which have been unfortunately committed on both sides.[15]

After receiving the information that the Governor of Rangoon had, through the petition of the merchants, agreed to all the terms and

> having regard to these considerations I entertain some hope, that if in reply to the Governor's letter these concessions should now be demanded as a ultimatum, they would be full made, and harmony might be restored.[16]

Lambert had not pressed for these terms and still he was not removed. Lord Dalhousie continued to rely on the Commodore's assessment of the situation at Rangoon, and with every despatch he told the Government of India that the Burmese had hostile designs. However, Colonel Bogle, the Commissioner of Tenasserim, who knew the Burmese and their language intimately, believed quite the opposite. He had received a letter from the King to be sent to the Governor-General and wrote in a covering letter to the Commodore:

> The circumstance of the Burmese Government having sent a letter to the Governor-General at all, and the speed with which it has come, would certainly indicate a desire that hostilities may be averted, at least for the present.[17]

The King, in his letter, asked Lord Dalhousie if 'Ka-mo-do Lan-bar' (Commodore Lambert) had been deputed simply to dispose of the question concerning the merchants 'or whether he has been sent to begin an atttack, which should have the effect of bringing on hostilities between the two countries'. It is tempting to suggest that Dalhousie retained Lambert as negotiator after his first disobedient act because the opportunity, though not of his making, was there to be seized, and that by retaining the fox in the hen coop it was only a matter of time before feathers began to fly.

It was all very well to castigate Lambert in the Blue Book, knowing as he must have done that these expurgated excerpts would not see the light of day for some fifty years, but if they did, there was Lord Dalhousie's condemnation for all to see. When it suited him, Lord Dalhousie said that Lambert was not under his authority, but in a letter to Lambert, Halliday wrote,

> you have stated in your despatch of the 31st January that 'the whole of the transactions that have taken place since your arrival at Rangoon have been forwarded to the Lords Commissioners of the Admiralty' and you add that 'to their verdict you must submit whatever it may be'. The Governor-General in Council is most reluctant to attach an unfavourable interpretation to any expressions employed by you. He therefore, feels assured that it cannot be the intention of an officer (whose aid was so readily afforded in the commencement and who has so zealously applied himself to the discharge of an irksome duty) to convey by those expressions the meaning they might be made to bear, namely that he does not admit the authority of the Governor-General in Council to pronounce upon his acts, when employed upon service under the instructions of the Government of India.[18]

Lord Dalhousie also had on his desk a letter from the Governor of Rangoon, again agreeing to make the payment demanded. In spite of the evidence he had of the Burmese desire to avoid a war with Britain, the Governor-General wrote in a minute on 12 February concerning the Governor of Rangoon's letter,

> far from making the required concessions, [he] has evaded them all...This letter leaves to the Government of India, in my deliberate judgement, no alternative but to exact reparation by force of arms.[19]

We are therefore left to wonder at his earlier expressed desire for peace between the two countries.

Lord Dalhousie's next act was on 18 February to send an ultimatum to the Burmese Court, containing the additional demand for £100,000, 'in consideration for the expenses of preparation for war, which he will agree to pay, and will pay at once'.[20] He then went on to threaten the King,

> [if] the King of Ava shall unwisely refuse the just and lenient conditions which are now set before him the British Government will have no alternative but immediate war. The guilt and the consequences of war will rest on the head of the Ruler of Ava.

The ultimatum was set to expire on 1 April 1852. Lord Dalhousie knew that the King, as an independent monarch, could not accept these terms. Indeed, five

days before he sent the ultimatum, he instructed Halliday, his Secretary, to write
to Lambert:

> The Burmese authorities having now finally rejected the demands that
> were last transmitted through you, the Government of India has deter-
> mined to proceed at once to exact by force of arms the reparation which
> it has failed to obtain by other means...[21]

The King was convinced that if he acceded to this demand, it would not be
long before another would follow. His half-brother, Prince Mindon, urged him
to accept the terms of the ultimatum and prevent war. In the end the King did
not reply. One cannot but wonder if because of his mental condition he ever
took an active part in these negotiations.

Richard Cobden was one of the few Englishmen who questioned Dalhousie's
actions. 'Britain,' he asserted, 'would not have acted in this manner towards a
power capable of defending itself.'[22] At the time Britain was engaged in one of
its periodic disagreements with America. Cobden asked: 'Why is a different
standard of justice applied in the case of Burma? Ask your own conscience,
reader, if you be an Englishman, whether any better answer can be given than
that America is powerful and Burma weak.'

The second Anglo-Burmese war commenced on 1 April 1852 when the
King failed to meet this deadline with a reply to Lord Dalhousie's ultimatum.
As a British naval squadron was already in place in the Rangoon River, all that
was required were troops and artillery from Bengal and Madras to commence
operations. Unlike the previous war of 1824-6, transport was relatively quick
by steamer and by 2 April 1852, the Bengal contingent had arrived with its
artillery. On 10 April they were joined by the troops from Madras. The military
were commanded by the elderly veteran of the first Anglo Burmese war, Lieutenant General Henry Godwin, and the naval force under Rear Admiral Charles
Austen.

Lord Dalhousie had learned the lessons of the first conflict and now left
nothing to chance. This time there were provisions in abundance and the finest
medical care. Prefabricated barracks of wood and bamboo for the officers and
men were produced in British-held Moulmein, ready for immediate shipping
when they had taken Rangoon.

Although British reinforcements were opposed all the way up the river to
the port, they made short work of the rather weak defences. The Burmese
gunners were no match for the ships' heavy guns firing broadside after broadside into the stockades which, although impregnable in medieval warfare, were

Plate 29 (right, top).The Burmese army behind their stockades on the Hlaing or Rangoon River (1852).
Plate 30 (right, centre). British warships storming Rangoon (1852).
Plate 31 (right, bottom). A captured Burman war canoe at Rangoon. *Circa* 1852.

now hopelessly out of date. The main defending army fell back to a stronger stockade centred around an ordination hall called Thein-byu, which was known to the British as the 'White House', next to the Shwe Dagon pagoda. At first, this fortification proved to be invulnerable until two twenty-four pounder howitzers were brought into play. Some of the Burmese regiments, about 800 strong, were also deployed on the pagoda platform. These men fought with great determination, inflicting nearly 150 casualties on the British, including 17 deaths. Captain Latter led the storming party, having received information that the eastern entrance to the pagoda was the least defended. Within the hour the position was taken and the Burmese were in retreat. Pearn commented: 'So Rangoon was taken in a manner which reflects nothing but credit on the courage of both attackers and defenders.'[23]

Plate 32. General Godwin who
defeated the Burmese in 1852.

On 5 April 1852 the ancient Mon port of Martaban, opposite Moulmein, fell; followed on 19 May by Bassein, another port. With the loss of Rangoon, the Burmese Court was deprived of any access to the sea. By June, Lord Dalhousie was advocating the annexation of the province of Pegu. This, with the two acquisitions of Arakan and Tenasserim from the first war would reduce Upper Burma (as it was soon to be called) to a landlocked kingdom. It would have become totally dependent on the goodwill of the British for its imports and exports, which had to move on the Irrawaddy through British territory. This was the ideal situation which the Rangoon merchants had envisaged.

General Godwin was therefore instructed to take Pegu, a small town about fifty miles (80 km) from Rangoon, and despite considerable opposition it fell on 5 June 1852. Nevertheless, the Burmese did not give up easily, and the town had to be retaken on 21 November. Lord Dalhousie wrote that 'they had heavy work of it since the Burmese had entrenched themselves closely in the jungle'. A garrison was placed in the town which was subject to continual harassment. Eventually they were besieged and had to be relieved by a force under General Godwin. To Lord Dalhousie's intense annoyance, Godwin had still not taken Prome, the last pocket of resistance in the Province of Pegu, and the town that had to be taken before annexation could be declared. Indeed at one time he thought of dismissing him. He wrote of the veteran:

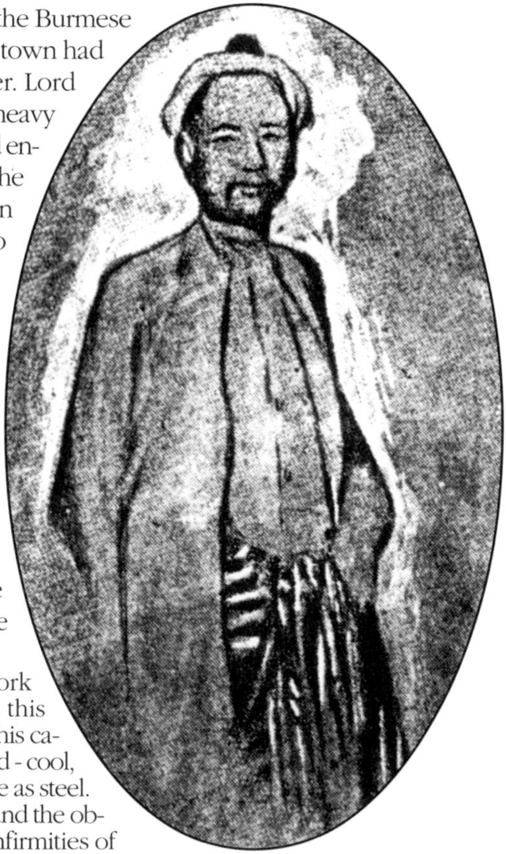

> No man stood harder work than General Godwin in this war; no man has disputed his capacity when fairly in the field - cool, rapid in his plans, and brave as steel. But he has the prejudices, and the obstinacy, and some of the infirmities of age; and these have made him slow to move, wrong-headed, and dilatory in undertaking operations where the qualities I have praised above would have been

Plate 33. The ex-commander Maha Bandula the Younger (U Kyan Gyi) who fought the British in 1852.

shown...As it is, I believe we shall bring all to a close; but if we do, the success will be due to the hand of God rather than to the sword of man.[24]

Hall depicted Godwin as a 'sort of blundering old fool' when he described his violent antipathy towards the navy, without which he could not have operated for a day. He relied on it not only for the transport of his troops, but also for his supplies and for its heavy guns. He was unwise enough to voice his thoughts in an official letter to the Government of India and was gently rebuked for his intemperate outburst. When Admiral Austen died, Godwin was furious, as this meant that Lambert, as the senior naval officer, took precedence over him as the Acting Commander-in-Chief of the Naval Forces in the Eastern Seas. He went so far as to say that he would not sign a peace treaty with the Burmese if Lambert's name appeared before his.

Although the area around Prome was being defended by Maha Bandula the Younger, the inexperienced son of the legendery Maha Bandula of the First Anglo Burmese War, the city fell on 15 October 1852. On 20 December, Captain Phayre, the Commissioner designate, announced the Proclamation of the Annexation of Pegu. It took until 30 June 1853 for a cease fire to be declared. And so this ' inglorious war', as *The Times* described it, came to an end and Britain had acquired another rich province. Was this what Dalhousie had intended? Not perhaps quite from the start, for if he is to be given the benefit of the doubt, he was being honest when he wrote to his friend Sir George Couper on 23 July 1853 that:

> there is no doubt that Lambert was the immediate cause of the war by seizing the King's ship, in direct disobedience of his orders from me. I accepted the responsibility of his act, but disapproved and censured it. He replied officially that he had written home, and was sure that Palmerston would have approved! However, I gently told him that while acting for this Government he must obey its orders, and we have never ceased to be good friends. ... But while I say this, I do not mean that but for his act the war would not have been. On the contrary, I believe everything would have been just as it has been.' [If not Lambert, then someone or something else?] 'Lamberts service during the war has been admirable. It is easy to be wise after the fact. If I had the gift of prophesy, I would not have employed Lambert to negotiate. But being only mortal, recognising the benefit of having negotiator and commander in one, if possible, and having to act through an officer of high rank not under my authority, I can't reproach myself with a fault in employing him though war did follow.[25]

So how did the principal participants gain from this squalid affair?

Lord Dalhousie, already an Earl and a Marquess (his preferred spelling), and a Knight of the Thistle could not look for any further material reward. He was content to pursue his imperialist agenda 'and was ready at all times to extend the frontier of his Indian domains'. This he did by conquest, annexation and by the use of what was called 'The Doctrine of Lapse'. This device was of dubious legality; dubious because it was devised by and only for the benefit of the East India Company. When the head of a princely state had no heir he could apply to the Governor-General for permission to adopt one, or after his death his senior relative could make such application. If successful, that person would be formally recognized by the Company. But by refusing such applications, Dalhousie

Plate 34 (right, top). The fortified town of Prome, with a British gunboat on the right (1852).
Plate 35 (right, centre). 'Interview between the Burmese Envoy and British Commissioners at Prome.' (1853).
Plate 36 (right, bottom). General Godwin shown leaving Prome (1853).

was able to add the Indian States of Berar, Sattara, Nagpur, the Carnatic, Tanjore and Jhansi to the Company's possessions. It should be noted that the case of Jhansi was one of the chief causes of the Indian Mutiny of 1857. Lord Dalhousie took the Punjab and Pegu by conquest, and annexed the Indian State of Oudh, remarking as he did that 'our gracious Queen has 5,000,000 more subjects and £1,300,000 more revenue than she had yesterday'.[26] This must have pleased him, since he had previously written 'the King of Oudh seems to be disposed to be bumptious. I wish he would be. To swallow him before I go would give me satisfaction'.[27]

However, he was well aware of the feelings expressed by some of the British newspapers, when he wrote ironically

the young Nawab of the Carnatic died suddenly a week ago. He has left no son, and it will be another windfall for the Company, and another text for abuse

Plate 37. A Burman soldier of the lower ranks.

of my insatiable rapacity and inordinate ambition.[28]

On the other hand, Lord Dalhousie was a man of prodigious industry, for he carried out many reforms benefiting both Indian and European: from the sanctioning of the remarriage of Hindu widows to the introduction of the railways and the telegraph into India. He died at the tragically early age of forty-eight years.

Major-General Sir Henry Thomas Godwin, KCB, CB, (1784-1853) who had fought inthe First Anglo-Burmese War of 1824-6, was not the most energetic of commanders and seemed content to carry out Lord Dalhousie's instructions rather than display any initiative on his own. Indeed, on more than one occasion, Lord Dalhousie had reason to be dissatisfied with his tardidness, which was not to wondered at in a man of sixty-nine. He is described as Lieutenant-General, which indeed he was, but due to an error by the Commander-in-Chief, was along with others reduced by one rank, probably a unique distinction for a commander in the field. He died in India before receiving the notification of his knighthood.

Commodore Lambert (died in 1869) was promoted to Commodore 1st Class and entitled to fly a red pendant. Lord Dalhousie wrote that 'he stands alone in the honour. The General [Godwin] and the Admiral ([Austen] won't like it much; but it is quite right, and I rejoice in it'.[29] On the death of Admiral Austen, Lambert became Commander-in-Chief. Dalhousie wrote,

> this is a wonderful piece of good fortune for our friend the Commodore. Most men's luck only clears the way before them; his clears every obstacle away before and behind him! It makes him Commander-in-Chief, with large allowances; antedates his chief command to Rangoon, as far as honours are concerned, and enables him to post his pet commanders and to make his son commander in his room! He well deserves it all, and everybody will rejoice in it.[30]

Plate 38. A Talaing (Mon) soldier

Sir George Lambert, KCB, Admiral of the Blue, retired on 5 March 1864.

Regarding Captain Thomas Latter (1816-53), 67th Bengal Native Infantry, there appeared to be something dark and sinister about this scholarly but sadistic officer. His captaincy was a brevet rank. Possibly it was his gift for languages, especially Burmese, that put him, as a comparatively junior officer, at the centre of things. That he was a brave man is beyond doubt. He was a Burmese scholar, an authority on the coins of and tribes of Arakan, and wrote three learned articles on these subjects; one for the prestigious *Journal of the Asiatic Society of*

Bengal and the others for the Royal Asiastic Society. In 1845, his *A Grammar of the Language of Burmah* was published. He also compiled and had printed in the Burmese language *Selections from the Vernacular Buddhist Literature of Burma* in 1850 in Moulmein. This was later translated by Captain Sparks under the title of *Decisions of Princess Thoo-Dammasari*, and printed in 1851.

After the war in 1852, his first preferment was to be appointed Magistrate of Rangoon, where his addiction to the rattan (cane) as a means of punishment soon came to be remarked upon. A Bombay newspaper reported in October 1852:

> Talking of Captain Latter, I may state, that Lord Dalhousie is said to have put a check up on his rigorous proceedings in his capacity of Magistrate, especially in regard to corporal punishment, in which he so much delighted. Of course the natives, Bengallees, Burmese, etc., are rejoiced at it.

The Moulmein Times noted in December 1852, that Captain Latter was to be one of the Assistants to the Commissioner of Pegu (Captain A.P. Phayre). His next promotion, in January 1853, was as Deputy Commissioner of Prome. It would appear that he was unsuited to the position, and began to write alarmist letters to the Governor-General, fortelling the defeat of the British in Burma.

Hall, in his edition of the *Dalhousie-Phayre Correspondence, 1852-6*, wrote that 'Captain Latter's letters of warning increased in number and intensity to such a degree that at last Lord Dalhousie could stand it no longer.'[31] His extraordinary credulity of alarmist rumours, which were proved to be absolutely baseless, aroused the 'deep disgust' of Lord Dalhousie, who threatened in September 1853 to remove Latter from his post. But things took a nasty turn and on 8 December 1853, Captain Latter was discovered dead in his bed, murdered. His throat had been cut and he had two wounds in his chest. His body had been covered by a woman's *htamein* (skirt); in the eyes of the Burmese for this to be done to a male was the ultimate insult.

Robert Samuel Edwards was made Collector of Customs for the Port of Rangoon. In 1874 he was appointed to the first Municipal Committee of Rangoon. This was an impressive rise in status for someone who was described by Pearn as being 'apparently of negro blood, and said to have been once a slave'. A pencilled note in the author's copy of Pearn's *History of Rangoon* claims that he was an 'Anglo-Indian Madrassi'. Edwards died in January 1877, aged seventy-six years, forty of which had been spent in the Company's service.

CHAPTER V

PROMISES AND THREATS

In 1852, when news of the carnage wreaked by the British on the Burmese army reached Amarapura, Prince Mindon tried to pressurize the King into opening peace talks. This interference, however, was not to the liking of the ruling clique and war party whose leaders were secretly syphoning off state funds for their own ends. At Court this was considered to be one of the perks of one's position and was indulged in even during the first war of 1824-6. The military moved swiftly and ordered the arrest of Mindon and his brother Kanaung, both of whom then escaped to Shwebo and raised their war standards. On 18 February 1853, Magwe Mingyi, the Chief Minister, having changed sides, seized the Palace and deposed the King who was by now incapable of ruling. He held the capital until the arrival of Mindon who then ascended the throne. All the troops in Lower Burma were recalled to the capital. King Mindon (r. 1853-1878) immediately released all the European prisoners and sent two Italian priests, Father Domingo Tarolly and Father Abbona, to contact General Godwin to say that he was sending a peace mission to halt the war and enter into peace negotiations. On their arrival, the two priests were told that it was too late and that the war had been unilaterally ended by the British who had annexed the province of Pegu on 20 December 1852.

Since it was undecided where the new boundary began, Captain Phayre, the Commissioner of British Burma, made his own, not at Prome where the last action had taken place and beyond which the British had not penetrated, but at Myede some fifty miles (80 km) further up the river. Phayre commented 'what prevented an advance to a more suitable and healthy site for a cantonment and the inclusion of a rich belt of teak forest in British territory?'[1]

For a time, Mindon naïvely hoped that the British would relent and return the annexed territory, but his envoys were firmly told that the proclamation was irrevocable. They were then invited to sign a draft treaty agreeing to this, and to the extension of the extra distance which Phayre had added as a clause to the original proclamation. This extra claim was so outrageous that even that firebrand, Commodore Lambert, together with General Godwin, could not agree with it, and said so openly.[2] Nevertheless, the frontier was fixed at six miles (9.6 km) north of Myede, but no treaty was signed as Mindon was adamant that he would never put his signature to a document that gave away territory.

Mindon, realising the difficulty of his situation, sought to keep open contact with the Governor-General and the Commisioner of British Burma, to which end he appointed a Scot, Thomas Spiers, as a liaison officer. Spiers, who was from Kirkaldy, was a well-liked and affable merchant based at Amarapura. He had married Ma Cho, a Burmese lady. Although he did not escape imprisonment with the other foreigners at the begining of the war, he seemingly bore no ill will towards the administration.

Spiers also received payment from the Governor-General as a go-between, and was one of the few merchants who was honest and impartial. Indeed he was able to convince Lord Dalhousie that Mindon had no intention of renewing the war, despite the constant rumours put about by the merchants and business men in Rangoon to that effect. Such rumours were invariably embellished by the missionaries; as usual the acquisition of converts, few though there were, was bitterly contested between the Catholics and Protestants. For the Protestants the fall of Mindon would give them the upper hand, whereas his continuence on the throne with his freedom from religious bigotry was beneficial to the Catholics.

Mindon made one more attempt to persuade Lord Dalhousie to relinquish Pegu, but this the latter adamantly refused to do. He probably felt that since the war had cost the British exchequer about £1,000,000 he had better have something to show for it. Nonetheless, Lord Dalhousie still wanted his treaty, or rather the Company did, and sent a mission to Amarapura to try to obtain one in 1855. The composition of the mission is worthy of comment. It was headed by Phayre, who had now been promoted to the rank of Major; the Secretary was Captain Yule, who spoke Burmese and was an expert on fortifications; Major Grant Allen, who was to gather information on all military questions connected with Burma and to report on the route to the capital; Captain Rennie, to investigate the Irrawaddy above Myede; and Professor Oldham, to discover the mineral resources of the country, especially any deposits of coal in the Ava area, just the sort of information which would be very useful to an intending invader. The mission was also accompanied by Colesworthy Grant, the artist; Captain Linnaeus Tripe, the photograher; and Dr John Forsyth, whose interest was the sanitary condition and natural products of the country. Mr Edwards was appointed attaché and interpreter. However, at the capital Mindon would not sign the treaty, ending all argument by saying that it was 'contrary to [the Burmese] custom'.

Meanwhile, in British Burma all was far from quiet, as the anticipated rejoicing with which the British thought they would be received by the Mon and Karen once the Burmese yoke had been removed, did not materialize. On the contrary, both groups rose in revolt, as did many Burmese, foremost of whom was Myat Htun, a former minor office holder at the capital but now variously described as a guerrilla, dacoit or opportunistic robber. Captain Loch RN was the first to underestimate Myat Htun and lost his life and his guns in an attempt to capture him. More than 80 men were killed or wounded in this ill thought out action. These weapons were subsequently turned on General Cheape when

Plate 39. Portraits of King Mindon and his brother the Crown Prince (1854).

he attacked the rebel stronghold, causing the death of 2 officers and 15 men, among those wounded were 10 officers and 90 men. Later, accompanied by 1,100 soldiers, a twenty-four pounder howitzer and rocket tubes, Cheape finally drove Myat Htun from his stockade, although it took him twenty-four days to achieve this. Such encounters doubtless revised the views of the British soldier on the ability of the Burmese as fighting men.

Phayre became so concerned at the lawlessness and anti-British demonstrations that he applied to the Goveror-General, that he

> should have the power of trying summarily all persons who may be found with arms in their hands, within the districts of Sarawah and Prome, opposing British authority civil or military, and be empowered to carry out a sentence of death in such cases upon those persons whom I consider it necessary to make an immediate example of.[3]

This power was given with the consent of the Governor-General and his Council. Gradually, due to the tenacity of Phayre and the superiority of the British forces, the rebel leaders were defeated, allowing the British to persue their overriding desire which was trade.

By 1860 conditions in Upper and Lower Burma had reached a degree of normality and trade was passing between them. Mindon had set up the nearest thing to a free market economy in his country, reserving only the right to tax imports and exports, much to the annoyance of the British traders at Rangoon.

In 1862, on the instructions of the new Governor-General, Lord Canning, Phayre was sent to Mandalay, Mindon's new capital, to discuss a commercial treaty, the success of which must have exceeded his greatest expectations. The treaty provided for the freedom of travel for British and Burmese on either side of the border, fixed rates of taxes on goods, and most important of all, authorized British merchants to proceed up the Irrawaddy into Burmese territory 'in such manner as they please without hindrance and to purchase whatever they require and to settle in any part of Burmese territory'.[4] The King also gave Phayre permission to send a survey mission to explore the caravan route to Yunnan through Bhamo. Phayre described the treaty as 'highly favourable to British interests'. The back door to China was at last open.

Early in 1863, Dr Clement Williams, an army surgeon was allowed by Mindon to visit Bhamo where he made enquiries about the routes to Yunnan. Although the Chinese whom he met told him that trade was impossible at that time due to the Panthay (Chinese Muslims) rebellion, his mission was not a complete failure, since he found that it was possible to take steamers further north than Bhamo on the Irrawaddy.

Lord Dalhousie had introduced the railway into India in 1854 and there had been talk at the time of it being brought to Burma with the Chinese trade in mind. Unfortunately, the kingdom of Upper Burma was in the way and the King's consent had to be obtained to pass the railway from Rangoon through the Shan States to the Mekong or the 'Upper Cambodia River' near to the frontier of Yunnan province. No doubt, had he been able to exact a tax on goods passing through his country he would have been more than happy to give permission, but this was precisely what the traders wished to avoid. Another alternative was to go through Assam to Yunnan, thus incidentally providing a source of cheap Chinese labour for the tea planters.

More worrying to the British were the rumours that the French in Mandalay were planning a railway from China through Burmese and Siamese territories. Meanwhile, trade still depended on the Irrawaddy, and the Government of India decided to invite tenders from private companies to supply transport for freight and passengers on the river with regular services and stated prices. In May 1864, Messrs. Todd, Findlay and Company received the contract and formed the Irrawaddy Flotilla Company. Dr Willams, who knew the river well, resigned his commission and became the Mandalay agent for the company.

The British continued to make incursions into Burmese territory in the hope of finding another viable route to Yunnan, and an expedition was duly sent to the Shan States, some of which were at war with Mindon. It was headed by two army officers who attempted to explore the Salween River, but to their cost it soon proved to be unnavigable for much of its length. Nevertheless, the pair held discussions with the Sawbwas (Shan chiefs) who ruled the territories through which they passed. Pearn remarked

> that the circumstances gave the Burmese officials [who questioned them] very good grounds for their suspicions; what after all, would have been the attitude of any officers in British Burma who found a party of Burmese officials entering their district in similar conditions?[5]

Not surprisingly, the two officers were ignominiously escorted back to Mandalay. The Chambers of Commerce in Britain and Lower Burma, however, continued with their relentless demands for the extension of trade with China, pointing out that the French might well open a trade route up the Mekong River to their detriment.

In August 1866 two of Mindon's sons, Prince Myingun and his brother Prince Myingondaing, rose up in rebellion and killed their uncle Prince Kanaung, the Crown Prince. During this incident they even tried to kill their father. Failing in this and finding the army against them, they seized one of the royal steamers and fled down the river to British Burma. Curiously, the two were allowed to continue their plotting in British territory. The younger of the two, Prince Myingondaing died of a fever, but the other was allowed to leave and go to the Karennee States to encourage the people to rise against his father. It was only when he had failed in this enterprise that the British arrested him and sent him to internment in Benares. The Governor-General, Sir John Lawrence, noted that 'all our merchants and traders long for a bouleversement and would probably do what they could to bring one on'.[6]

Mindon now urgently needed arms, as he was facing revolt not only by some of the Shans who were favourable to the cause of Prince Myingun but also by treacherous elements in his army who wanted the son of the assassinated Crown Prince to be King. But since he had no access to the sea, the King could only purchase weapons from the British who controlled the ports. With this in mind, he invited the Governor-General to send a commercial mission to Mandalay. A mission headed by the new Commissioner Albert Fytche duly arrived at the Burmese capital in October 1867. He later reported that he had the friendliest reception and obtained all the commercial concessions he had sought, including the appointment of a resident at Bhamo and permission for the Irrawaddy Flotilla Company to send a boat to Bhamo once a week. In return, Mindon was to be allowed to buy arms. The treaty read:

Plate 40. General Sir Arthur Phayre, Commissioner of British Burma.

The Burmese Government shall further be allowed to purchase arms and ammunitions and war materials generally in British territory, subject to the consent and approval in each case, of the Chief Commissioner of British Burma, a note was added to the treaty which said that such consent and approval would ordinarily be given.[7]

The King also obtained a separate agreement for the purchase of arms from Fytche. What Fytche did not discuss with Mindon was the suggestion from the Governor-General that the following clause be inserted into the treaty:

The Burmese ruler engages not to enter into negotiations or communication of any kind with any foreign power, except with the consent, previously obtained, of the British ruler.[8]

Agreement to such a proposal would have made the independent kingdom of Burma virtually a British Protectorate which would have met with the approval of Lord Cranbourne, the Secretary of State, who wrote to the Governor-General,

> it is of primary importance to allow no other European power to insert itself between British Burma and China. Our influence in that country [Upper Burma] ought to be paramount. The country itself is of no great importance. But an easy communication with the multitudes who inhabit Western China is an object of national importance.[9]

Once the starting gun had been fired, Colonel Sladen, the Resident at the Burmese Court, was off to Bhamo wearing his other hat as an employee of the British companies in Rangoon. As they had put up the money for his expedition, his aim was to make trade agreements with the Chinese and to use Bhamo as a base for shipping the goods down to Rangoon, thus excluding Mandalay. As far as Sladen was concerned, the annexation of Upper Burma was inevitable, but tiresomely delayed.

In March 1869 Captain Strover of the
Madras Staff Corps was appointed
Assistant Political Agent at Bhamo,
acting under the direction Sladen.
He was very soon pursuing
Sladen's policies of visiting or
sending missions to the Shan
and Kachin chiefs most of
whom were not well disposed
to Burman rule. The idea
was to point out to them the
virtues of the British, and
their wish to bring trade and
prosperity to these states, in
comparison with the Bur-
mese, who merely wanted to
keep them subjugated. As
evidence of his good intent he
occasionally sent presents of
guns to the chiefs. Despite Mindon
asking for his part of the treaty to
be honoured so that he could buy
guns and ammunition, Chief Commissioner Fytche repeatedly refused
his request. The King soon realized

Plate 41. Lieutenant-General Albert Fytche, C.S.I.

that he had been outmanoeuvred by the British, and that he would obtain no
satisfaction from the Governor-General who would support his Chief Commissioner. It was only in 1881, after Mindon had been dead for at least three
years, that Lord Ripon (Governor-General of India) declared that in this the
British were guilty of a breach of faith.

It had always been a sore point with the Burmese that they had to deal with
a governor-general, a mere appointee, rather than the king or queen of Britain.
Mindon was further humiliated when he found out that even petty rajas and
chiefs in India were able to write to the Queen and the Secretary of State and
always received courteous replies. And so in 1871 Mindon wrote to Queen
Victoria and obtained a reply and a gold watch. He then decided that as an
independent sovereign he would send a diplomatic mission to England. In 1872,
the Kin Wun Mingyi (First Minister) led the first mission to England.

The British authorities were furious, as they saw it as a slight not only on the
Resident at Mandalay, but also the Chief Commissioner at Rangoon and the

Governor-General in India. Had Fytche not been on leave, he believed that he could have stopped the mission as he had when a similar one to France that had been proposed in 1867. The Kin Wun Mingyi had been warned by the Government of India that no political matter was to be discussed with the Government of Britain. Fytche declared that 'the mission would be regarded solely as one of a ceremonial character'.[10] The attitude was that the Bur mese King was not to be regarded as a independent monarch, but subordinate to the Governor-General. The mission travelled via Cairo to Italy, where it was granted an interview by the King, and his Foreign Minister discussed a treaty of friendship and commerce. In France, the delegation was met by the Foreign Minister with great courtesy. On 5 June 1872, the Burmese arrived at Dover to a civic reception and a salute of nineteen guns was fired. In London they were greeted by the Duke of Argyll, the Secretary of State for India, and not the Foreign Minister, as any other independent countries' representative would have been. It was the intention that the Burmese were to be made aware that their dealings were to be through the Government of India and not with the British Government.

On Friday 21 June the envoys were received by Queen Victoria at Windsor Castle, where the opportunity to inflict further humiliation was eagerly seized upon. The envoys were required to prostrate themselves before the Queen and members of the Royal Family, as they would to their own king; no English envoy had ever been required to prostrate himself before a king of Burma. The next day they met the Prince of Wales and other members of the Royal Family, together with the Prime Minister, at a reception for ambassadors at St James's Palace. They then started out on a sightseeing trip of the country, where their entertainment was mostly provided by the Chambers of Commerce and the civic authorities of the towns they visited.

The envoys took every opportunity to present the Burmese view and especially to refute the suggestion that the King of Burma was reluctant to encourage trade through Bhamo. As one of the envoys pointed out to the Glasgow Chamber of Commerce, the opposite was the case. Mindon had been losing millions in revenue annually due to the fighting there between the Panthays and the Chinese. He also pointed out that this situation was not helped by the British refusing the King permission to procure arms to put down the lawlessness on the Burmese side of the border. The Kin Wun Mingyi took the opportunity when speaking to the Liverpool Chamber of repeating Mindon's desire to have direct relations with Britain. He said:

> Our relations with the Government of India have been cordial, but as
> you are doubtless aware there is a difference between dealing through
> agents and direct dealing through principals. It is our fond hope that in
> order to promote existing friendship and trade relations, we could get
> the approval of Her Majesty's Government to the appointment of a

Burmese Consul in London.

But this was obviously not going to happen, as the American Ambassador in London noted and wrote to his Government:

> There has been a 'Burmese Embassy' here... I think.. they were intelligent enough to observe that, although coming accredited to this court in a diplomatic character, their presentation to Her Majesty, and the delivery of their credentials, were under the auspicies not of the Minister of Foreign Affairs, but accompanied by the Secretary of State for India. There seemed a significance in this fact. It was as if the government here was willing to consider questions of relations with Burmah, as belonging to the policy which controls in regard to the eastern possessions of Great Britain, and not to the treatment which is to be given to an independent power.[11]

While the mission was in Britain, an embassy from the Panthay rebels also arrived in London. This gave *The Times*, no friend of Burma, the opportunity to inform its readers that: 'While showing every courtesy to the Burmese, we should remember that they have usually obstructed our trade whereas the Panthays welcome it.' The paper further suggested that the King of Burma had only sent his mission to outshine the Panthays. This was the result of the malicious propagana put about by Sladen. *The Times* reported that Sladen had been obstructed in every possible way by the Burmese in his attempts to get to the capital of the Panthays. But that he had, however, managed to reach Momein, where he found the Panthays kindly and tolerant.

Plate 42. Queen Victoria receiving the Burmese Embassy at Windor Castle (1872).

What Sladen had deliberately failed to mention was that he had gone to Bhamo with Mindon's permission, and that the King had ordered all officers within his territories 'to further the progress of the English party by every means in their power'. He also did not refer to his speech to the Royal Geographical Society in London, in which he said 'the expedition itself reached a point in China as far as, and beyond that to which the discretionary powers with which it was invested permitted'. And finally, he failed to tell *The Times* that it was only because Mindon had given the Panthays safe conduct through his country, risking the wrath of the Emperor of China, that the Panthay embassy was in London at all. By then, the Kin Wun Mingyi could see that his mission to London had failed. The British would not for a moment countenance an accredited representative of whatever rank from the independent state of Upper Burma. Nevertheless, hoping to retrieve something, he decided, while waiting to make a farewell call on the Queen as diplomatic usage required, to visit France, where the British Ambassador offered to present his group to the French authorities! The offer was politely declined. The Kin Wun Mingyi signed a commercial agreement allowing for the exchange of diplomatic agents, trading rights and concessions and facilities for travel to Burma, with reciprocal rights for the Burmese. The British became paranoid about this treaty, and fearing that there might be secret clauses, stopped a French envoy who was passing through India to Mandalay to get the treaty ratified, and demanded a firm assurance that the French had no political interest in Burma. In the event, the treaty was not ratified, possibly because Mindon feared the British reaction. Meanwhile, there was no shortage of ideas in Britain as to the route that should be used to bring the wealth of China to the British dominions in India. One was to link the Irrawaddy with the Brahmaputra River in eastern India (by road or rail) whereby the trade from south-west China could go to Calcutta as well as Rangoon. When Dr John McCosh, the well-known military photographer addressed the British Association in Bradford, his tone well typified the feelings of the time:

> When the prodigious commerce of the Indus, the Ganges and the Brahmaputra, the Ning-llee [Chindwin], the Irrawaddy and the Yang-tse-kiang shall be hoisted on trucks and rolled from east to west, from west to east in one grand tide, ever ebbing, ever flowing, everlasting, and when London and Liverpool, Manchester and Bradford, Glasgow and Paisley, Dundee and Aberdeen shall dip their pitchers in the sacred stream and deal out its bounty to the people of the land.[12]

One of the wilder schemes proposed was a viaduct over the mountains between the Irrawaddy and the Brahmaputra.

In 1873 the Panthay rebellion in Yunnan ended with the Chinese regaining control, whereupon the Governor of Yunnan immediately restored trade with Burma. This caused the Irrawaddy Flotilla Company to double its service from

Mandalay to Bhamo to accommodate the extra business. But for the British authorities there was always the shadow of the French, who having acquired territories in Indo-China were also exploring the possibilities of trade with Yunnan from Tongking. For the British, what can only be described as a stroke of luck occured when Augustus Raymond Margary, a young interpreter who had made a unique journey from Shanghai to Bhamo overland, was killed by some Chinese. This gave Mr Wade, the British Ambassador, just the stick with which to beat the Chinese into giving concessions. As a result, a large indemnity, changes in taxation, and trade facilities were all obtained through the threat of war. He also required that British officers should be able to go anywhere in China to support British subjects where their person or property were at risk. Permission was also obtained for the acceptance of consular officers in China. All this and more was agreed to in September 1876.

Meanwhile, Mindon had to deal with trouble in the Karennee and Shan States. It should be remembered that when Britain annexed the Province of Pegu, it came into contact with the Karennee State. This region was ruled by two chiefs, one in the east and the other in the west, over both of whom the kings of Burma held sovereignty. After the war of 1855, when a British survey party entered Western Karennee to determine the frontier, the chief, Koontee, claimed that at the time it was independent of Burma. Lord Dalhousie accepted this, and without querying its reliability arbitrarily ruled that since he would not take the State, the Burmese should not have it either. This, however, did not prevent Sladen from interfering. He secretly encouraged the chiefs to look towards the British and was soon urging the Government of India to take the State of West Karennee:

> If the British Government possessd the state we would have a complete check over the Eastern Karennee,[whose chief Tsawlawpaw, was loyal to Mindon] and obtain a richly populated country giving us direct access to Yunnan through the friendly Shan States.[13]

Mindon made a futile attempt to have his claim to Western Karennee recognized by the Government of India, and although a mission headed by Sir Douglas Forsyth was sent to discuss the matter, Dalhousie refused to waive his demands. This clearly shows that the British were prepared to go to war if a treaty was not signed to the effect that Mindon recognized the independence of Western Karennee. The King could see that the British were looking for an excuse to invade his domain and reluctantly agreed to the loss of another portion of his territory, thereby accepting further humiliation.

It was after the return of this mission that Sir Douglas Forsyth complained to the Government of India of the indignity of British officials having to remove their shoes before having an audience with the King. This form of court etiquette was something which all Western officials had accepted up to then, however reluctantly. The complaint had an immediate effect. Orders were is-

Plate 43. A rare portrait of King Mindon dated 1873.

sued that the British Resident in Mandalay was not to remove his shoes when he next appeared at Court. Mindon, on hearing this, promptly refused to receive him. This meant that further personal contact with the British was now no longer possible a situation which continued until the King's death in October 1878 at the age of sixty-four.

Regarding the 'Shoe Question'as it became known, it should be pointed out that like the Japanese and other Oriental races, it was not the custom for the Burmese to wear shoes indoors; footwear was always left outside the main door. To appear unshod in the presence of royalty and ecclesiastics was a mark of respect and good manners. But the British attitude was that hundreds of years of royal protocol, for which the Burmese had an unusual obsession, be set aside so that their envoy might keep his shoes on in the king's presence. On becoming Governor General, Lord Ripon commented that the shoe question was a petty one and that the British could have found some compromise had they wished to.

It is thought that the cause of Mindon's demise was dysentery, which was often a long and painful illness, and in those days invariably fatal. Unlike others of his dynasty, Mindon was a religious and benign monarch. As a devout Buddhist he convened the Fifth Great Buddhist Synod in Mandalay and built numerous pagodas and monasteries. He even paid for the construction of an Anglican church in Mandalay and a rest house for pilgrims at Mecca. During his reign he instituted many changes which were to the benefit of his people. Among other things, he introduced coinage, and instituted a uniform system of weights

Plate 44. King Mindon in his Palace at Mandalay (1876).

and measures throughout his kingdom, both of which resulted in an increase in trade. He kept taxes down to 10 per cent of a person's annual income. Mindon put the remuneration of officials on a proper footing, thereby preventing them from imposing extra taxes to maintain themselves. Promising students were sent to Rangoon and Calcutta to learn to operate the telegraph system, and on their return instituted the telegraph throughout Upper Burma. By joining this to the British system, contact was made throughout the world. He funded the establishment of many small factories for the production of textiles, wheat, rice etc., much to the annoyance of the British merchants, to whom local manufacture was anathema.

This brief resume of his achievements is no bad epitaph for an 'oriental despot'. Even Yule had to recognize the King's qualities, albeit grudgingly. He commented,

the King is, without doubt, a remarkable man for a Burman, but rather in moral than in intellectual character, though his intelligence also, is above average... He is, in fact, as far as we can judge, a man of conscience and principle. The very monopolies of trade which he has established in his own behalf have been created with the intention (however shortsighted) of securing a revenue without the infliction of taxation on his people...There can be no doubt about his personal popularity. The people speak in terms of admiration of his good qualities, and uniformly, and with apparent sincerity, declare they never had a king so just and so beneficent. The contrast with what they have known heretofore, by experience or by tradition, must be powerful.[14]

CHAPTER VI

EVENTS LEADING UP TO THE ANNEXATION

W ithin the *shwe-myo-daw* ('golden city') of Mandalay, the month of October 1878 had been a fraught one for its inhabitants. Mindon had finally succumbed to his illness. Over the years he had acquired 63 recognized Queens, numerous concubines, 48 sons and 62 daughters, many of whose thoughts now turned to surviving the bloodbath which was expected to follow. Although there was a succession procedure it was ignored by those in power, which meant that each prince could be a possible contender, for the eldest was not generally recognized as the heir apparent. Understandably, such a haphazard situation was positively explosive, and in the past had resulted in the successor killing all his male siblings whom he considered a threat. As we have seen, before Mindon's death, although his younger brother Kanaung had been appointed Crown Prince, he had been assassinated by two of his nephews, the Princes Myingun and Myingondaing who were naturally resentful at being barred from the succession. This tragic turn of events prevented Mindon from nominating another, saying that it would be equivalent to signing that person's death warrant.

In the Palace, the power struggle had already begun, for Mindon's illness lasted three months and the conspirators had ample time to plot. The principal schemers were the forceful Queen Sinpyumashin (Mistress of the White Elephant); the Kin Wun Mingyi who was the senior Minister in the Hlutdaw or Privy Council; and the Taingda Mingyi, Minister and head of the Palace Guard and Intelligence Service and described as a vicious ruffian. Queen Sinpyumashin secretly issued orders to all the adult Princes to attend their dying father, and when they appeared had them arrested. Fortunately Prince Nyaungyan and his brother Nyaungok had been warned and escaped to the S.P.G. mission, from where they were taken by the Rev. Mr Colbeck to the British Residency. Mr Shaw, the Resident, then smuggled the two princes and their families in his gunboat to Rangoon. They were later transferred to Calcutta and maintained at the expense of the Indian Government.

The remaining Princes were not so fortunate. When their detention became known their distraught mothers rushed to the King's chamber and informed him. Mindon immediately ordered the Princes' release and had them brought before him. To prevent further trouble he rather unwisely announced that the kingdom be divided into three provinces, each to be ruled by one of his three senior sons, while the junior Princes could follow whoever they wished.

This was a recipe for disaster and would have led to civil unrest. Sinpyumashin, however, was having none of this, and as soon as the Princes left their father's apartment, she had them re-arrested and their mothers confined to their own quarters.

On the death of Mindon, Sinpyumashin, now Dowager Queen, summoned the Ministers and firmly presented as her choice the Prince Thibaw. The naïve twenty-year old was one of Mindon's younger sons who had virtually no claim to the throne. He had spent most of his youth in a monastery where he had achieved academic success. She pointed out to her co-conspirators that Thibaw was malleable and furthermore was under the thrall of her domineering middle daughter, who was to become notorious as Queen Suphayarlat. The Dowager Queen also had plans to marry off Maing Naung Suphayar and Yamethin Suphayar, her eldest and youngest daughters to Thibaw, thus consolidating her position at Court. Such an arrangement may now sound bizarre but it was common practice among Burmese royals for half brothers and sisters to marry, thus keeping the line pure. Full siblings, however, were excluded from this tradition.

The Ministers were finally persuaded and accepted the Dowager's plan, although each for different personal reasons. The Kin Wun Mingyi agreed because he had visited Europe and as a result of his experiences wanted to make constitutional changes and to put Burma firmly into the nineteenth century; the Taingda Mingyi, because he wished to maintain the status quo. Both thought their influence would achieve their aims, but they wer e both to be sadly mistaken.

Once Thibaw had been crowned, the Dowager Queen showed her true colours. She and her daughter, Suphayarlat, persuaded Thibaw that it was necessary to 'put away' (a euphemism for execute) all of the Princes and Princesses who might challenge his claim to the throne. This was an age-old custom and had been practiced in the past as a means of preventing factional rebellions and civil war. It also maintained the king's hold on the throne. The last time such a massacre had taken place was in 1846 when Pagan Min succeeded his father Tharrawaddy. On the other hand, Mindon was the first ruler to break with this tradition when he came to the throne. As a devout Buddhist he would not allow it.

In February 1879 while Thibaw, his Queens and court watched lavish theatricals, some eighty members of the royal family were herded together well away from the merrymakers and ruthlessly murdered. Young and old alike were either strangled or clubbed to death by criminals released from the Mandalay jail for the purpose and fortified with alcohol. This method of execution was dictated by an ancient taboo which forbade the spilling of royal blood. A similar practice also existed in Thailand, where pieces of sandalwood were used as clubs. After the slaughter, the bodies, dead or unconscious, were thrown into a trench, the earth filled on top of them and trampled down by elephants. The killers are said to have perpetrated the most frightful excesses on the numerous attendents of these unfortunate royals.

News of the killings spread and Mr Shaw, the horrified British Resident, made a strong protest which was officially ignored. Nevertheless, the Ministers became alarmed when they saw the British reaction to the massacre and the threat of the withdrawal of the Resident if the slaughter continued. This no doubt saved some lives, although many were to remain in prison throughout Thibaw's reign which ended in 1885. The new administration was also worried that the British might use the killings as an excuse to invade the country, and so sent troops to the frontier. The British, too, did the same.

Doubtless, Britain would have invaded had she not had her hands full elsewhere: there was a war in Afghanistan, another in South Africa against the Zulus, and signs of trouble with the Boers. As the military explained to the Government, although it would only take a few troops to annexe Upper Burma, many thousands more would be needed to pacify the country after the event. It soon became obvious that Anglo-Burmese relations were deteriorating under Thibaw, and the merchants in Rangoon seized on the killings as the perfect excuse for annexation. They claimed that they were horrified by the recent news. This of course was sheer hypocrisy since it was a matter of indifference to them how many of his subjects Thibaw slaughtered.

When the Burmese Ministers saw that there was no response to their actions and realized that Britain was hard pressed on other fronts, they decided that the time was right to give the lion's tail a little tweak. In Mandalay there were a number of small anti-British incidents culminating with a crowd of hooligans insulting the British Assistant Resident. Although these events were not necessarily instigated by the Ministers, neither were the offenders punished.

In June 1879, Mr Shaw, the Resident, died at Mandalay of a heart complaint. Such medical conditions are often accompanied by feelings of chronic apprehension, but whether this was true in Mr Shaw's case cannot be known. He always expect the worst and lived in constant fear of assassination.

> The correspondence with poor Mr. Shaw in 1879 is very humiliating reading. He was regularly in the lion's den, and he used to beg that not a man should be sent to his help, as the first sight of a British uniform across the frontier would be the signal for his decapitation.[1]

This was a rumour that had been started by the Rangoon merchants.

Mr Shaw was replaced by Colonel Browne, the first to contend that Thibaw was a drunkard. This calumny was never substantiated by any other officer; indeed, just the opposite. In 1885 when Thibaw was being taken into exile, the officers on the ship offered him all sorts of liquor. If ever there was a time when a man might have taken a drink that was surely it, but he refused all alcohol.

Plate 45. The Burmese army at Mandalay (1879).

Colonel Browne also reported that the Kin Wun Mingyi, who was losing his influence to the Taingda Mingyi, was ready to throw in his lot with the exiled Prince Nyaungyan, Thibaw's half-brother. He also claimed that the Dowager Queen, that arch-schemer, was prepared to marry her eldest daughter to Nyaungyan should he ascend the throne. How Browne obtained this information remains a mystery, but it is possible he accomplished it through carefully placed spies in the Palace.

This about-face by the Dowager Queen was due to her having been elbowed out of the way by the autocratic Suphayarlat, who in 1882 had taken complete control of the government. Her authority was described as *dah-htet-te* (as sharp as a razor). Although Thibaw had married all three sisters, and had designated the eldest as Chief Queen, she had been removed and confined to the Dowager Queen's apartments on Suphayarlat's orders. The two sisters did not get on. Suphayarlat was vindictive and had become the terror of the Palace. According to Pagan U Tin, *ah-htauk-daw* (spies) swarmed everywhere and reported everything to Suphayarlat. She even had her mother under surveillance. In 1886, Lord Dufferin, in one of his letters wrote that a court lady had told him that when Suphayarlat 'lifted up her little finger, the whole city trembled' and that her cruelty exceeded all belief. Those who crossed her tended to meet an unpleasant end.

Curiously, just at this time, Prince Nyaungyan was permitted to visit Rangoon. He was on hand as it were to marry the Dowager Queen's eldest daughter, receive the support of the Kin Wun Mingyi, and with British assistance be placed on the throne as a puppet. But he soon returned to Calcutta. It is tempting to wonder if Browne was not flying a kite here, and that this was what the British desired. After his useful, if albiet short tenure of office in Mandalay, and seemingly without the fear of instant death, Browne returned to Rangoon and was replaced by a chargé d'affaires, Mr St Barbe. Hall said that St Barbe

> lived in a state of continuous blockade: no Burman dared be seen
> entering or leaving the Residency, and there were persistent rumours
> that Thibaw contemplated a massacre of its inmates. Actual prepara-
> tions for such a deed were made several times during 1879.[2]

It is inconceivable to any detached observer that the above could consist of anything but rumour and speculation. The Burmese knew that to kill the Resident would result in the British seeking immediate and bloody revenge. Even had they contemplated such a course of action, and knowing its result, they would surely have mobilized the army and the people, but no, the state was quite tranquil.

Strangely enough, what the British feared might happen in Burma occurred in Afghanistan. On 3 September 1879, Sir Louis Cavagnari, the British Resident at Kabul was murdered, together with his brother and all the other British officials. Although St Barbe was instructed to withdraw immediately, it was not until 7 October that he finally left. So much for the threat in Mandalay!

Thibaw, of course, had not been told of the reason for the departure of the Resident, an appointment the British had insisted on since the Treaty of Yandabo in 1826. Sensing trouble, he sent an embassy to the Viceroy to ask for the return of good relations; in effect, the reinstatement of the Resident. The embassy reached the frontier at Thayetmyo but was not allowed to proceed by the Hon. Ashley Eden, the Chief Commissioner of Lower Burma. As far as the British were concerned, Thibaw had to be put firmly in his place. Firstly, it was claimed that the embassy had no powers to negotiate, but this was immediately remedied when Thibaw invested the envoys with plenipotentiary powers. Next, it was claimed that to allow the embassy to go to Calcutta would give it too high an opinion of itself. The matter of the treatment of the Resident was then raised, and the dissatisfaction of the Viceroy voiced as to the treatment of Shaw and St Barbe. Whereupon the Burmese envoys agreed to accept a British Resident in Mandalay with all due ceremonial. Then came the question of the King's monopolies. The envoys said that all these matters were within their purview, but still the Chief Commissioner raised difficulties. Eventually, the Burmese realized the impossibility of their situation and returned to Mandalay. Possibly, the resolution of the difficulties did not suit the plans of the Viceroy. Indeed, it seemed that Lord Hartington, the Secretary of State for India, was being kept in the dark. He wrote on 17 September 1880:

Plate 46. King Thibaw, Queen Suphayarlat (centre) and her sister Suphayarglay (1886).

As your Excellency in Council will have gathered from my telegram of the 10th of July, I was in the first instance disposed to doubt whether the absolute rejection of the Burmese overtures, resulting in the return of the embassy to its own country was altogether judicious. It appeared to me that although the Ambassador might not have been authorized to make the specific concessions desired by the Government of India, he had been funished with general powers sufficiently to justify continuence of negotiations, and that the personal discussion which was sought might possibly have led to a satisfactory result. The question, however, is one in regard to which the deliberate judgement of the local authorities is entitled to great weight. In view, therefore, of the conviction entertained by the late Chief Commissioner, shared apparently by your Excellency in Council, that the King's overtures were insincere and illusory, I am not prepared to dissent from the course that has been adopted.[3]

Throughout 1881, Viceroy Lord Ripon and the new Chief Commissioner Mr Charles Bernard continued to try to get a commercial treaty signed at Mandalay, while the merchants of Rangoon were clamouring for something to be done. Pearn wrote

with the deterioration of relations after the accession of King Theebaw, however, the suggestion that political control over Upper Burma should be enforced was revived, and the English merchants in Rangoon played a considerable part in an agitation to this end.[4]

The two treaties of 1862 and 1867 had lapsed and so too, argued the Ministers, had the restrictions on the King's monopolies; and in any event the British had dishonoured the 1867 treaty by not supplying arms to the King.

Much has been said of the King's monopolies and possibly an explanation would be helpful. The kings of Burma were autocratic monarchs, the country and all its people in effect belonged to them. At the time Thibaw reigned the whole of Upper Burma was his personal property. He owned the ruby, amber, jade and silver mines, the teak forests, and the oil wells. It was only at his pleasure that he allowed others to work them and to pay him a tax on their revenue. Thibaw, as an absolute monarch, levied a tax on everything exported from his country, such as ivory, tea, cotton, and palm sugar. Only in this way and by these taxes could the country remain solvent. He had to pay the army for the security of the country and the ministers and officials to administer it. He also had many religious endowments to support. He had to maintain his court with its innumerable personnel and hangers on and, with it, his dignity before his subjects. He was further beset by internal factional fighting with dissidents (encouraged by the British) in Eastern Karennee and the Kachin and Shan States, and with Chinese guerillas in Bhamo. Indeed, he was obliged to fight off Prince Nyaungok, who the British had allowed back into Rangoon and who with some followers had managed to buy arms and invade parts of Upper Burma. But having failed in this, the Prince was sent back to Calcutta. Had he been welcomed with open arms by the populace, no doubt the British would have further encouraged him.

The merchants at Rangoon wanted an end to these royal monopolies, while at the same time perversely maintaining their own. They had a monopoly over the rice and textile trade with Upper Burma and set the prices to their own satisfaction in Rangoon. If the King's agents wanted to buy, then that was the price. One can imagine their rage when they found that Thibaw's agents were buying rice direct from the farmers in Lower Burma and textiles from the markets in Calcutta. It would seem that the audacity of a sovereign king in a sovereign state deciding where he bought his groceries and haberdashery astonished them.

The merchants further complained that Thibaw was being obstructive in the matter of an overland trade route through Upper Burma to China. This in their minds became synonymous with El Dorado, and so great was the outcry of these merchants that Lord Ripon was obliged to visit Rangoon in December 1881 to tell them personally that he would not go to war with the Burmese just to extend their trade. However, some move had to be made to placate the mercantile community. Accordingly, to the Burmese on 4 January 1882 Bernard wrote:

> If the Government of His Majesty the King continue the policy of monopolies, the Viceroy and Governor-General of India will be compelled to regard the Government of Mandalay as indifferent to the maintenance of good relations with the British Government.[5]

On the 16 February, Thibaw abolished the monopolies and sent an embassy to India to discuss a new treaty. Unfortunately, due to intransigence on both sides these negotiations came to nothing and the Burmese envoy was recalled to Mandalay. Next, the Ministers sent two draft treaties to Calcutta, which they must have known would not be acceptable. This was no doubt the work of the Taingda Mingyi; he and the imperious Suphayarlat were both strongly antipathetic to the British. As a result the situation deteriorated as the wise influence of the Kin Wun Mingyi had become eclipsed. Possibly, as a form of compensation, the by now elderly Minister had been created Mingyi-thet-taw-she (one who could not be killed out of hand by the king – a dubious title) and was still nominally the Commander-in Chief of the army. The weak and inadequate Thibaw was being advised by his strong-willed wife Suphayarlat, the Dowager Queen, and in particular the Taingda Mingyi, a minister dependent on their favour and ardently pursuing his own ends.

These personalities little realized that they were playing dangerously with fire and were soon to be badly burnt. Despite subscribing to newspapers from Rangoon and India, they were incapable of comprehending the prevailing British policy which Sir Alfred Lyall described in his *The Life of the Marquis of Dufferin and Ava*. He wrote that

> ... it has always been the policy of the British-Indian government to prevent any other European Power from obtaining a foothold within

Plate 47. The Burmese embassy to the Viceroy of India. Envoys dressed in their military robes of state (1882).

the Asiatic States situated on the borders of our actual possessions. Just as a fortress or a line of entrenchments requires an open space around or in front of it, so it is manifestly advantageous for the security of a kingdom to be surrounded by a ring of territories with which powerful neighbours must not meddle. Upon this principle we place the adjoining States under our protectorate, whether they desire it or do not; and thus our political influence radiates out beyond the line of our actual possession, spreading its skirts widely and loosely over the lands adjacent. From the time when the British dominion was established in India, the prosecution of this policy has been one leading motive of wars, annexations, and alliances.[6]

Chapter VII

The Prelude to the Third Anglo-Burmese War, 1885-6

The British had been looking with ill concealed annoyance at French expansionism in what came to be known as French Indo-China. In 1862 the French had annexed three provinces of Cochin-China. The next year they ejected the Siamese from Cambodia and declared it a French protectorate. This was followed in 1867 by the remainder of Cochin-China being occupied. Hanoi was seized in 1883 and Laos was soon to follow.

At Mandalay, Thibaw decided to send an embassy to Europe in 1883, ostensibly to gather information about European arts and sciences. In fact it was an attempt to sign treaties of friendship and commerce with France, Germany and Italy. Thibaw and his advisors could see that they were getting nowhere with the British, as they still did not have an Ambassador at the Court of St James's they were being forced to deal with the Viceroy like any petty raja in India. They knew, too, that they were never going to be able to purchase the arms needed to restore order in the country.

The British response to the Burmese embassy to France was predictable. Lord Lyons, the British Ambassador to France, told the French Foreign Minister and President of the Council, M. Jules Ferry, that Britain had a special interest in Burma and would have strong objections to the conclusion of a treaty between Burma and a foreign government of anything other than a purely commercial nature. The British Foreign Secretary, Lord Kimberley, showed his concern in a minute where he wrote,: 'I do not like what is going on in Paris with these Burmese, and fear there is trouble in store for us.'[1] Such fears were, of course, whipped up by the mercantile community in Rangoon where the Chamber of Commerce provided a clearing house for rumours, no matter how far fetched. These were then relayed to the Chambers in Britain who petitioned the Government.

By 1884 the trickle of rumours had increased to a flood. Some were plainly foolish, such as that the French were going to establish a flotilla company on the upper Irrawaddy. For what purpose? Or that the French were proposing to build a railway across the Shan States, linking French Indo-China with Mandalay. This would have been technically impossible at the time. Or that Thibaw was about to lease the fabulous ruby mines to a French company. Had he done so, the loss of face before his subjects would have been unsustainable. In their eyes it would have amounted to him declaring that he was incapable of managing a royal monopoly.

Other rumours were more viable: that Thibaw proposed to have a clause in the commercial treaty with France in order that he might buy arms; that he was negotiating with other European states in order to reduce his dependency on the Government of India; that he was asserting his rights as an independent king to make treaties with whomsoever he chose. This last was not at all to the taste of the merchants and traders at Rangoon, who at a public meeting in the Town Hall in 1884 resolved to urgently petition the Government of India to annexe Upper Burma. Interestingly, the minutes of their meeting record that it was attended by 'an immense concourse of Burmese, Europeans, Chinese, and Natives of India'.[2] The *British Burma News* (the local newspaper), however, reported that no more than five persons of position were present from the non-European community. In fact the Burmese held their own meeting and resolved not to interfere in foreign affairs, and to concern themselves with the prosperity of Lower Burma. Unfortunately, in the middle of 1884 Thibaw and his advisors unwisely decided to massacre the remainder of his half-brothers, their numerous followers and those of the exiled Princes. This merely gave extra ammunition to the merchants of Rangoon who could now claim God on their side in the person of the Reverend Dr Marks, the leading Anglican churchman in Rangoon. Marks did not cease to preach on the iniquities of his former pupil King Thibaw.

In 1884 too, money was raised by the Rangoon merchants and sent to Prince Myingun who, having escaped captivity in Benares in 1882 by what the Burmese considered dubious means, had taken up residence in French Pondicherry. Although the merchants urged the Prince to foment a rebellion in Upper Burma, the French would not allow this and kept him under close supervision, since they undoubtedly had their own plans for him. But as far as the Government was concerned, even under protectorate status the volatile Myingun, as a creature of the French, could not be entertained for the position of ruler. Of the two Princes Nyaungyan and Nyaungok who had escaped Thibaw's massacres, the elder, Nyaungyan, died early in 1882, ending the hopes of some of the Burmese and Rangoon merchants of replacing Thibaw with another member of the royal family. His surviving brother was not considered suitable.

Thibaw's embassy to Europe, which had begun in 1883 and lasted into 1885, resulted in a French treaty, and one with Germany of peace, friendship and commerce. It also maintained diplomatic relations with Italy which had been negotiated by the Kin Wun Mingyi during his visit in 1873. However, it was the treaty with France that concerned the British, and it is there that the waters became very muddy. On the one hand there was the Prime Minister of France telling the British Ambassador that the treaty between his country and Burma had been of a purely commercial nature and contained nothing political or military; on the other there was a document obtained by the Italian consul, Chevalier Andreino, from a clerk in the Mandalay Palace (presumably a translator), in which M. Ferry agreed to supply arms to the Burmese through Tongking. Surely fate smiled on the Chevalier that day. He was, in addition to his diplomatic appointment, the agent of the Bombay Burma Trading Corporation and the Irrawaddy Flotilla Company, and as Htin Aung avers, the head of the British spy ring at Mandalay.

The correspondent of *The Times of India* wrote on 2 November 1885 that Mr Andreino was served well by Palace spies who he had to reward liberally. Not a discussion took place between the Burmese Ministers and M. Haas (the French Consul) of which a complete report was not furnished to Mr Andreino. He obtained copies of the original draft treaty before they were funished to M. Haas and enabled the Chief Commissioner to telegraph the contents to the Secretary of State before the French Government obtained its copy of it. The writer concluded that by the time his despatch was published, Mr Andreino would be safely in Rangoon or be dead.

Hall confidently writes that M. Ferry had deliberately double-crossed the British Government. Conversely, Woodman takes the opposite view, quoting Lord Salisbury's meeting with M. Waddington, the French Minister in London. On putting the charge to him,

> His Excellency replied that he knew nothing of the alleged concession, and had heard nothing of the kind...He said that when he himself was Foreign Minister, a similar offer had been made to him with respect to the affairs of Burmah and that he had absolutely refused to maintain any communication with the applicant.[3]

Waddington added that he would discuss the matter with M. de Freycinet, M. Ferry's successor, and convey to him the British Governments concern. During the time M. Haas was in Mandalay, he had obtained concessions, or thought he had, for the establishment of a bank in Mandalay. They also included the building of a railway from the capital to the railhead in British Burma. More importantly, in return for the granting of loans, the management of the royal monopolies was to be taken over.

When this intelligence was received by the British, the French were told firmly that they could not and would not agree to any such concessions by any one other than themselves in Burma. Since the French were not prepared to fight for these concessions, they removed M. Haas 'for reasons of health'. In 1885 the new Government in France under Prime Minister M. de Freycinet still kept the pot simmering, despite a barrage of complaints and veiled threats from the British. Meanwhile, in Rangoon the merchants took full advantage of the situation to urge annexation claiming that trade had suffered under Thibaw and would suffer further if he were to give concessions to the French. In fact, the former was not true as the Chief Commissioner pointed out, trade had in fact increased since Thibaw's accession.

The Rangoon Chamber of Commerce began circulating Chambers in Britain, urging them to petition their Members of Parliament and the Secretaries of State for Foreign Affairs and India. Soon these officials were receiving a flood of letters. Pearn wrote:

> There can be little doubt that the pressure brought to bear by the Rangoon Chamber of Commerce and its corresponding bodies in Great Britain had a good deal to do with the willingness of the Imperial Government to bring Upper Burma under the British Crown.[4]

Official British feeling regarding the Burmese was well known at Mandalay, for Thibaw once remarked to Mr Moylan, *The Times* special correspondent, that his Ministers took the paper in order to find out English public opinion. They also subscribed to newspapers published in India for the same purpose. Contrary to later accounts of this period, the Court was in fact well informed. Lord Randolph Churchill, the Secretary of State for India, was in complete agreement with the policy to annexe Upper Burma, while Bernard, the Chief Commissioner, was not. In 1855, Churchill made the subject of Burma a matter for the Parliamentary elections, and toured the country giving speeches extolling the benefits to be gained by annexing Upper Burma. He concentrated in particular on the manufacturing centres whose goods he claimed would be welcomed in the vast new emporium. When the Tories were returned and Churchill was appointed Secretary of State for India, he set about redeeming his election pledge. In this he was opposed by Mr Bernard, the Chief Commissioner of British Burma, who wrote:

> If King Theebaw's Government transgressed British frontiers, invaded British allies, maltreated British subjects, broke treaties, continued to commit massacres, rejected British projects, and refused redress, matters would be different. But things have not come to any such pass.[5]

It would appear that Lord Dufferin, the Viceroy, agreed with his Chief Commissioner. He wrote to Lord Kimberley, the Secretary of State:

> We have been urged to annexe Upper Burma or to dethrone the present King, and establish another ruler protected by us. These measures however do not appear to us to be justified by the existing state of affairs, and the commercial community have been so informed.[6]

However, in the India Office, the determination to annexe Upper Burma continued unabated. Sir Owen Burne, Lord Randolph Churchill's secretary, wrote to his counterpart in the Foreign Office,

> ...I feel quite sure that some far more absolute action that we are not yet aware of must be taken in India. I say unhesitatingly that we should now get any pretext to annexe or make Burma into a protected State. King Theebaw's sins are many and great and I feel quite sure your able

Plate 48. The state barge of a minister (1885).

pen, aided by a few snarls from myself could formulate a Bill of indictment against him that would make every old woman in London weep.[7]

As it so happened, the very excuse for intervention was to drop into the hands of Lord Randolph Churchill. Since 1864, the Bombay Burma Trading Corporation, a company of British merchants, had contracted with the Burmese Court to extract timber from the vast forests in the interior. But the cordial relations between the two suddenly took a turn for the worse in 1885. Sir George Scott put the matter succinctly:

> The Corporation had been working the Nyingyan [now Pyinmana] forest under three separate contracts; the contract of 1880, under which the Corporation undertook to pay the King for all timber extracted from the forests at fixed rates per log; the contract of 1882, established the payment of a lump sum of one hundred thousand rupees annually for the right to extract the inferior and under-sized timber, which the Corporation was entitled to reject under the earlier lease; and thirdly, the contract of 1883, by which the Corporation undertook to pay a lump sum of one million, four hundred thousand rupees annually, from October 1884, for all timber not unsound or under four and a half feet in girth, extracted from the forests.
>
> The Burmese Government confused the contracts together; counted logs twice over; accused the Corporation of bribing the Governor of Ningyan [it was claimed that he had conspired with the Corporation to understate the number of logs extracted]; endeavoured to persuade the Corporation's foresters [these were Burmese, and were to claim that they had been underpaid] to come to give false evidence in Mandalay; tried the case without giving the Corporation opportunities for defence; issued judgement ordering payment to the King, by way of duty and fine, of sums aggregating over nine million two hundred thousand rupees, and to the foresters sums totalling about two million

Plate 49. A Burmese General (1885).

rupees; and dispassionately professed to have based their decision entirely on figures obtained from the British Forest Office in Toungoo. All logs contained in these lists were taken to be full sized; no account was taken of the lump sum contracts, and the money totals were wrongly added up to the extent of sixty thousand rupees in the king's favour.[8]

Hall was to take this a stage further and claimed that the case was brought against the Corporation because a French syndicate was being formed to take over the forests and would have paid an increased revenue to Thibaw. Bernard, the Chief Commissioner, felt that he did not have sufficient information to give an opinion whether or not the Corporation owed the King's Treasury more royalty than their local agents estimated. The licences, he said, were not precisely worded and they had worked favourably for the Corporation. He added that it might turn out that the Burmese Government had equitable claim, but such a claim could not amount to the fine imposed. He seemed to imply that if a little thievery went on then it was not to the amount alleged by the Burmese. Understandably, a somewhat different interpretation was put on these events by Htin Aung. He claimed that the case was brought by the foresters who contended that they had been underpaid for the number of trees that they had felled and floated down the river to the Corporation's saw mills at Toungoo. They produced their lists in support of their claim. The Corporation also produced its own lists, showing a significantly smaller number of logs, on the basis of which they had paid the foresters.

The court before which this matter came could not, of course, reconcile these two disparate lists and decided to take one list, that of the Forest Office at Toungoo which recorded the number of logs received there. This was agreed by both parties and the Chief Commissioner. Subsequently, when a list was drawn up under the Corporations seal, of the logs received at Toungoo, it revealed a considerable discrepancy between the number received and the number paid for by the Corporation. The Corporation then claimed that many of the logs which made up the deficit were short logs, and therefore the full price was not paid for them. The foresters, however, said that no short logs had been supplied, and nowhere on any of the three lists did mention of short logs appear.

Htin Aung's version of events was based on Burmese official court records, and it is interesting to note that the Corporation did not seek to deny the short payment but merely to offer the excuse that the logs were of less value than that claimed. The discrepancy was 57,955 logs and the Corporation was ordered to pay the foresters £33,333, and fined £36,666. According to Burmese law, any short payment of revenue was doubled, so the total costs to the corporation was the very hefty sum of £106,666. Even assuming that all the logs were short and payable at half price, the fines would still have been considerable.

Plate 50. Lord Dufferin, Viceroy of India.

The British Government was furious that an indigenous court had imposed a fine on a British company for at the very least, apparently sharp practice. That, together with the thought that the French had or were about to play some part in the enterprise encouraged them to actively consider annexation. Before this, however, the Viceroy, Lord Dufferin, suggested that the case go to arbitration and that the arbitrator to be appointed by him! Not surprisingly, the Burmese declined his offer. Needless to say, the merchants in Rangoon could not have been more delighted at this turn of events. Their compatriots in Britain now had even more ammunition with which to lobby Lord Randolph Churchill, who really needed no lobbying at all, merely an excuse, and this was it.

The Times of India wrote on 26 February 1885:

> The Bombay-Burmah Trading Company will hardly, says 'The Pioneer' [a sister paper] be gratified by the light esteem in which their rights against King Theebaw are regarded by Mr. Gladstone when

Leader of the Opposition. Indeed they may be thankful that other considerations, such as French intrigues, have intervened, for Mr. Gladstone has intimated very strongly that he would otherwise have lent the whole weight of his influence to prevent the application of force to redress their wrongs. This is no new doctrine with Mr. Gladstone. Throughout his career he has been the strongest opponent of the principal that a British citizen settled in a foreign country is entitled, when wronged, to the full support of his Government. It is doubtless both inconvenient and costly to have to protect the rights of every English trader or missionary who may venture into savage countries, and we may find it necessary to impress on such adventurous spirits that they must go there at their own risk. But if, notwithstanding this, they get into difficulty, the instinctive obligation which prompts the national guardian to help them out of it is hard to resist.

Lord Dufferin subsequently sent an ultimatum to the Burmese Government, the very words of which rang hollow.[9] It contained five points:

1. That an envoy be received at the Court at Mandalay, without submitting to any humiliating ceremony. (This must have produced a wry smile on the face of the Kin Wun Mingyi, as he remembered having to prostrate himself before Queen Victoria.)

2. That no action was to be taken against the Corporation pending the envoys arrival.

3. That a British agent must be permanently stationed at the Burmese capital, with a proper guard of honour, and a steamboat for his protection

4. That the Burmese Government was to regulate its external relations in accordance with British advice.

5. That British trade was to be opened up between China and Bhamo.

The ultimatum was sent on the 22 October 1885 and a reply was demanded by 10 November.

Earlier, in a private letter dated 19 October 1885, Lord Dufferin had commented:

This attack upon the Burmah Trade Corporation seems to have originated in a desire of Theebaw's Minister [Taingdar Mingyi], who is a savage brute, originally belonging to Theebaw's father's bodyguard, to obtain money for his master, the ladies of the harem, and himself, and it looks as though in their folly and ignorance the Burmese were determined to rush upon our bayonets...[10]

The Times of India published an article by its correspondent on 5 November 1885 of an interview he had had with Prince Nyaungok, the surviving brother of Nyaungyan:

Naturally, I turned quickly to the question of peace or war. Prince Nyaungok declared at once and without hesitation his belief that Thibaw would fight rather than submit to the terms of the ultimatum. He remarked that the position of a king in Burmah was very peculiar. 'The

Plate 51. The Devonshire Regiment about to attack a dacoit stronghold.

King of Burmah is regarded by the nation with great veneration, and according to Buddhist religion is the representative of the deity, and for the king to humble himself before his subjects would be to strike a blow at their faith. This I am aware the British do not intend, but to annexe the country would in the eyes of the people, amount to the subversion of the Buddhist faith.' The prospect of such a catastrophe, he thought, the people of Burmah would never submit to without a struggle, even if they dispaired of the result. I suggested that, perhaps Thibaw might be guided by a sense of self interest. This idea he rejected. His firm belief was that Thibaw had neither the inclination nor the power to submit. 'If he has the sense of his ancestors he will fight against any odds. I know, and you too know the Burman character. To become a mere creature and puppet of a foreign state, keeping up an empty show of power upon tolerance, and suffering daily humiliation in the eyes alike of ministers and people - for this is how the matter must present itself to Thibaw - is a fate to be resisted to the last. Even if Thibaw was craven to his faith, it is more than his life is worth to surrender.' The force of the opinion seems to me irresistible, and although it is specially hazardous to predict the turn of the wheel at Mandalay, I am inclined to believe the Prince's views will be borne out by events.

According to Htin Aung, Thibaw's agent in Rangoon sent a report that the British would insist on a special envoy being received, who would not only be wearing his shoes, but also his sword; it was an inviolable rule that no one

appeared armed before the King. There was to be a British guard for the Resident of 1,000 soldiers, and a steamer with enough cannon to destroy the royal
Palace.

It must come as no surprise that Thibaw could not agree to these stipula-
tions as it would have reduced his country's status to less than a protectorate. If
the British were to govern his external relations, it was only a matter of time
before the Resident would be 'advising' on his internal relations with the diverse
tribes which made up his kingdom. More and more British soldiers would be
sent to keep him in power, until he had served his purpose and then he would
be forced to abdicate. For the Burmese, to fight was the only honourable thing
left, although the result was a foregone conclusion. Meanwhile 10,000 British
troops were sent to Rangoon, ready for an immediate march on Mandalay should
the ultimatum be rejected, which they knew full well that it must be.

Chapter VIII

The Looting of Mandalay Palace

In answer to the ultimatum, Thibaw sent a reply saying that the case against the Corporation had been tried in accordance with Burmese law and that if the Corporation rejected the findings, 'they could petition him on the subject and he would be pleased to look after and assist foreign merchants and traders, so they should not suffer any hardship'.[1] Furthermore, he welcomed the appointment of a British Agent at Mandalay, and was willing to assist the British to increase trade with China. However, since he could not agree to conduct his foreign affairs in accordance with the advice given him by Britain, he suggested that this proposal be put to France, Germany and Italy, with whom he maintained diplomatic relations, to seek their views as to whether such a demand was reasonable. This, of course, meant the rejection of the ultimatum.

Almost as soon as the ultimatum had been sent, the Viceroy dispatched troops to Rangoon, from where they were moved up to Thayetmyo on the frontier. It would seem that the merchants and traders of Rangoon were at last reaping their first rewards. The Burma Field Force comprising some ten thousand men had to be fed from local produce, and when this was insufficient, supplies were sent from Calcutta. The Irrawaddy Flotilla Company chartered all its vessels for the transport of the troops up to Thayetmyo and ultimately to Mandalay. From the biggest to the smallest, what trader could have failed to make a profit? And this was just the beginning.

In command of the force was Major-General H. N. D. Prendergast, VC, who had seen much service and earned his VC during the Indian Mutiny. He was to have the services of Colonel Sladen as his Chief Political Officer, relieved from his duties as Commissioner of Arakan. The force consisted of three infantry brigades, one from the Bengal army and two from the army of the Madras Presidency. These were commanded by Brigadiers G.S. White VC, H.H. Foord and F.B. Norman. There were also three mountain batteries and three batteries of the Royal Artillery, together with six companies of sappers and miners.

At Mandalay, Thibaw issued a proclamation on 9 November 1885, telling his subjects that the British, having most harshly made demands calculated to bring about the impairment of our religion, the violation of our national traditions and customs, and the degradation of our race, are making a show and preparations as if to wage war with our State

He would, he assured them, take care of this matter, the people were to stay calm and not leave the country. It should be noted that during his chaotic reign, his subjects had been crossing the border in their quest to escape the harsh conditions and tyranny for a better life in British Burma.

On 11 November, Lord Randolph Churchill telegraphed the Viceroy: 'Please instruct General Prendergast to advance on Mandalay at once.' And so the might of the British army was directed against a weak sovereign state, not to save British lives but to protect British profits.

As the Burma Field Force moved up the Irrawaddy it was met with some fierce opposition especially at the forts at Minhla. The Burmese soldiers fought bravely, faced as they were with regular British troops many of whom may have seen service in Afghanistan, Egypt or the Soudan, with the result that the defenders were out-gunned, out-manoeuvered and out numbered. The Burmese continued to try to impede the progress of the flotilla up river at every opportunity, and a small engagement took place just beyond Pagan and again at Myingyan. On 25 November the flotilla anchored for the night a few kilometres further north at Yandabo, where sixty years earlier the treaty ending the first Anglo-Burmese war had been signed.

The journey up river had been unpleasent, as there was almost continuous unseaonable rain and cholera broke out among the troops who were crowded onto barges and flat topped vessels without any shelter. Soon they would reach the ancient city of Ava where it was anticipated a last stand by the Burmese would be made. While preparations for this were taking place events took a surprising turn. A state barge suddenly appeared with a flag of truce. The two Burmese envoys on board informed General Prendergast and Colonel Sladen that the King would now agree to all the points in the ultimatum and presented a letter from the Ministers which ended with the plea:

> The English Government entered our country and attacked us with a number of war vessels. We were obliged to resist. We now desire that hostilities shall cease, and we trust the English Government will meet us half-way and enter into a treaty, by which friendly intercourse may be resumed between the two great countries.[2]

Sladen's reply to this was that according to his instructions from the Viceroy, General Prendergast did not have the power to offer an armistice, therefore,

> no armistice can at present be granted, but if King Theebaw agrees to surrender himself, his army, and his capital to British arms, and if the European residents at Mandalay are all found uninjured in person and property, General Prendergast promises to spare the King's life, and to respect his family. He also agrees not to take further military action against Mandalay beyond occupying it with a British force, and stipu-lates that the matters in dispute between the two countries shall be negotiated on such terms as may be dictated by the British Govern-ment. A reply to this communication must be sent so as to reach General Prendergast before 4 a.m. tomorrow morning.[3]

Plate 52. The capture of the village of Minhla, with its fort. 2nd Bengal Light Infantry charging the enemy (1885).

In fact a reply did not arrive until 10 a.m., but for the British troops it was well worth waiting for, as it signified the end of hostilities. The reply which contained instructions to all the Burmese military commanders read:

> When the English ships arrive you are on no account to fire on them. Let all our troops keep quiet. Publish this abroad everywhere. The King concedes unconditionally all the demands made by the Commander of the English forces as contained in his letter (of yesterday's date). You are to let the English Commander know as quickly as possible.[4]

The British flotilla arrived at Mandalay at 10 a.m. on 28 November 1885. Colonel Sladen had told the Burmese envoy at Sagaing that it would 'expedite matters' if Thibaw should come with the Kin Wun Mingyi and surrender himself on board the General's ship. This was but the first of a series of studied insults. Not content with taking his country, the British, it seemed, were reluctant to allow him to keep even his dignity. When by one oclock neither the King or the Minister had arrived, the troops were disembarked. Sladen, accompanied by his clerk and interpreter Nicholas, and Commander Morgan, set off for the Palace. According to *The Times of India*,

> groups of Burmese collected in the streets traversed by the troops, but they turned out in no great number to witness the spectacle, and sat on their haunches, and smoked and gazed upon it with impassive countenances.

The British at last took possession of Upper Burma and its capital Mandalay, after a squalid little war which had lasted just eleven days. The editor of the *Bombay Gazette* described it as not a war at all, 'it was merely a street row. The

Plan of Mandalay c~1900

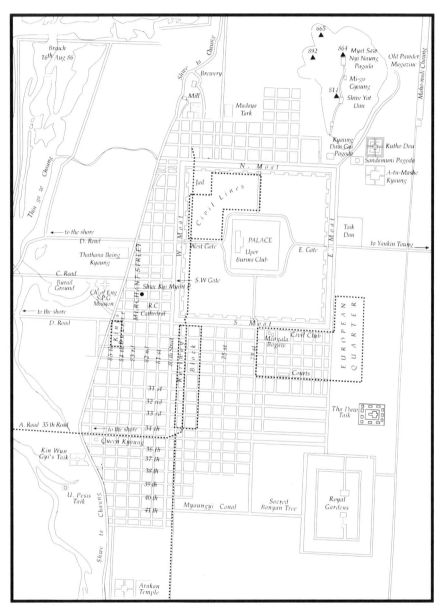

Plate 53. Plan of Mandalay c. 1900.

Plate 54. 'Entry of the British troops into Mandalay' (1885).

Burmans had not prepared for war; they never believed it would come.' Once within the walled city, Sladen and his group first went to the Hlutdaw, or Council Chamber, and were shortly afterwards received by Thibaw and Suphayarlat in the great Hall of Audience, where the royal couple behaved as if nothing untoward was happening. Although Suphayarlat was at her impressive regal best, it was noticed that the King displayed a slight nerveousness.

According to the *Konbaungset Chronicle*, when Thibaw was informed that the British soldiers had entered the Palace compound, he supposedly unsheathed the fabled *yein-ngwe-par-dah* (said to be an extremely flexible sword) and accompanied by members of his family and some of his ministers, went to face Sladen and his party. That the King appeared with a drawn sword is not recorded in any Western sources. But if he did think of arming himself while he was in his private apartments, he was no doubt quickly persuaded by his ministers not to do so as the British officers carried revolvers. The Burmese author, Sann Themain, who is renowned for his wild claims, asserted that it was the heavily-pregnant Suphayarlat who held the equally famous royal sword called *nan-thu-san-myeik* (sword-slim-as-a-court-lady's-hair switch) during the encounter with Prendergast. Such accounts must be pure propaganda as the fateful meeting was well documented.

During the interview with Sladen, Thibaw surrendered himself and his kingdom and asked if he might have time to prepare for his departure. He said that he would leave the Palace and go with his family into a summer house. In reply, Sladen informed him that General Prendergast was in supreme command, to

Plate 55. 'Deposition of King Theebaw – General Prendergast gives him ten minutes' grace' (1885).

carry out the orders of the Government of India. He added that neither the King nor his family would be interfered with within the Palace that night. Htin Aung, who had access to native sources as recorded by the courtiers present, remarked on Sladen's behaviour, for it had changed completely. His former subservient style had been replaced by an air of satisfaction. It was not surprising that he evinced some appearance of triumph as he strode about the Palace booted and giving orders, where formerly he had to ask for favours in his stockinged feet.

The next morning when Sladen introduced Mr Moylan, the Rangoon correspondent of *The Times* to Thibaw, the King told him that he had 'given up all the crown jewels, and I am sure that the English, who are a great people, will not object to me, as a King, keeping my ring, or my wife keeping her jewels'. Thibaw was referring to a magnificent ruby ring and a diamond necklace. Sladen agreed. So, at this point in 1885, as far as Thibaw was concerned the crown jewels were safe. Moylan in his despatch reported a night of looting, 'and the crown jewels only just saved by Sladen'.

At noon, when Prendergast arrived with his entourage to receive the King's submission, he said that Thibaw must leave the Palace within ten minutes, and that he was to be taken by steamer that very evening down river *en route* to India. A reporter from the *Illustrated London News* who was present, noted that Thibaw was seated at an opening on the low platform of the summer house and that he

> had no particular richness in his dress, and was, as far I remember without jewellery. The only royal appendage that I noticed was a huge gold spittoon, so heavy that it is said to take two men to carry it. In personal appearance he was stout, and looked heavy and unintelligent. The Queen [Suphayarlat] crouched behind the King in the orthodox Court position of respect. She was eagerly whispering to the King nearly all the time [the swords described by Burmese sources were not noticed beside them]. The Queen's mother, one of the wives of Theebaw's father, the only one, I suppose, who had escaped death or

Plate 56. King Thibaw being taken by bullock cart to the *Thooreah* waiting on the Irrawaddy (1885).

imprisonment, sat near her. We stood on the King's left, on the floor below him, our heads about level with his. To his right, the ministers who had accompanied us lay prostrate, with lowered heads, it being a great crime even to look at the King. He seemed in fear of his life, mainy, as I understood, from his own people, though this is probably an unnecessary terror. He had already complained of their [the Ministers] ingratitude, and seemed quite disgusted with them. His favourite servant, on whom he had lavished large sums, had run away the night before, and left him, I believe, even without food.

Htin Aung wrote that Thibaw asked if he could leave his city with some dignity as befitting an ex-king, either in a palanquin or on an elephant, but this request was rejected. Instead, he and his Queens were offered *doolies* (covered stretchers used to take the sick to the hospital). They naturally refused. According to the *Konbaungset Chronicle*, Mape-myosar, the Minister of Artillery and the Pyauk-myosar, the Treasurer, then arranged for two bullock carriages to convey the royal party. The Wet-ma-soot-Wundauk and the Pindale Wundauk, each holding a white umbrella, walked beside each cart; the female attendants belonging to the royal party and each carrying a huge bundle on their heads followed on foot. Thibaw and his family rode in the two bullock carts from the Palace and did not walk for 'several miles', as reported in a recent publication; there were also only two white umbrellas and not eight. The British troops formed two lines and the procession then passed out of the Palace city. So began the un-

Plate 57. King Thibaw about to board the *Thooreah* on his way into exile (1885).

comfortable four-mile (6.4 km) journey to the Gaw-wun jetty on the Mandalay foreshore. It was noticed that as the day wore on some of the attendants broke away and disappeared into the crowds taking the valuables with them (another fact never mentioned in Burmese sources).

Thibaw and his family were taken down to Rangoon on 29 November and three days later were on their way to India and eventual exile at Ratnagiri on the Bombay coast. *The Graphic* said that Theebaw had taken jewellery worth 400,000 rupees, and the Dowager about half that sum. Although these figures were based on official sources, it is not known what else was concealed on their persons. Among Burmese men and women it has always been the tradition during times of civil unrest to conceal portable valuables in the hem of either their *pasoe* or *htamein* (sarong). According to the mischevious Mr Moylan, in Mandalay the night of 29 November had been a disaster:

> Last night, the streets were occupied by gangs of armed Burmans who looted and murdered almost unchecked. The Princesses of the Royal Family were robbed of their jewels in the streets. [This is curious as many of the Princessess were still confined in prison and none lived outside the palace stockade.] The Buddhist monasteries were plundered [this, too, is difficult to believe as valuables were rarely stored within a monastery] the military arrangements to protect the town were very deficient.

Plate 58. Arrival of King Thibaw in Rangoon, where he and his family were transferred from the *Thooreah* to the *Clive* which took him into exile in India (1885).

While many of the vernacular newspapers in India were in favour of the deposition of King Thibaw and the proposed annexation of his country they were by no means united in this. On 22 December, *The Times of India* quoted from *The Indian Union*:

It must be exceedingly painful to those Hindoos who have not forgotten the old traditions of their race to hear the violation, in the case of King Thibaw, of the noble rule of chivalry...humility to foes conquered by valour is the only conduct becoming the brave. Humane and honourable treatment of a vanquished enemy was an essential feature of Hindu chivalry. A conquest was not taken advantage of by a Hindu warrior for indulging in bluster and swagger. It was an occasion on which he loved to give play to his generous feelings. Those who are bred in these traditions must have been moved to read the telegrams from the seat of war - if war it may be called - which describe the dealings of the General of the invading force with the fallen King of Burmah. It must be revolting to them to peruse the exulting messages which relate how British officers visited the King with their boots on, and how the King and his ministers submitted to this breach of etiquette; how the King was surrounded by guards at twenty paces from him; how he asked for time to prepare himself for his exile from the land of his birth and sovereignty, and how his captor replied that he

Plate 59. The British Army encamped within the Palace grounds, Mandalay (1886).

could not be allowed more than ten minutes; how the King and Queens were huddled in bullock carts; and how they were deprived of the melancholy satisfaction of hearing the parting wails of his subjects in the noise of triumphant kettledrums. We thought the British General could well have spared all this humiliation and mortification to the King after usurping his territory without any cause.

After the removal of Thibaw, two of his wives and two infant daughters to exile in India, there followed a period of uncertainty. It was unclear whether the British Government would appoint another Burmese prince as ruler under their protection, or reduce Upper Burma to the status of another Native State in the Indian Empire, or annexe it to the Queen's Dominions.

The merchants at Rangoon had by now become almost frantic in their demands for annexation, and on the 4 December the Secretary of the Rangoon Chamber of Commerce wrote to the Chief Commissioner:

...Imperial affairs, however, are for the consideration of statesmen, but so far as the matter is affecting British trade, the opinion of the British merchants should, we respectfully urge, carry weight; and as (Imperial consideration of frontiers apart), this matter is one only affecting British trade in general, and the welfare of this province in particular, the Chamber ventures to hope that Government will give due weight to the opinion of the mercantile community of Rangoon, whose local

Plate 60. A group of British officers in their temporary quarters in the Palace grounds, Mandalay. *Circa* 1886.

experience enables them to judge better than outsiders of what is best for the interest of the country; and who, next to the people of Upper Burma, will be most seriously affected for good or evil by the decision to be arrived at as to the future government of the higher part of the valley of the Irrawaddy...The Chamber maintains that every argument in the interests of the country itself and of British trade points to annexation as the best and only really safe and wise course to adopt.

To the merchants, it was vital that annexation and the melding of the two halves of the country take place, for if a separate protectorate or a native state were imposed they could foresee the imposition of customs and taxes. The merchants, had they known it, really had no worries, as Churchill was determined that Upper Burma should be annexed, and it was just a matter of time before he got his way.

On 1 January 1886, as a New Year's present to the Queen, the following proclamation was issued:

By Command of the Queen Empress, it is hereby notified that the territories formerly governed by King Theebaw will no longer be under his rule, but have become part of Her Majesty's Dominions, and will during Her Majesty's pleasure, be administered by such officers as the Viceroy and Governor-General of India may from time to time appoint.[5]

'A Dacoit Hunting Party with trophies, Myanaung.' Photograph dated 1886.

Plates 61 and 62.

Notorious dacoit leaders from the Henzada district who terrorized their own people. Shinbyan Boh, Boh Sein and Sangyan (standing left to right). Maung Pataw, Santhu and Nga Maung, shown seated, were hanged. Photograph dated 1886.

However, all was not peaceful in the newly acquired territory. Earlier, Moylan had noted that

> it seemed that General Prendergast had neglected to disarm the Burmese army before allowing them to disperse; being now unemployed many of them turned to dacoity.

As soon as the kingdom had fallen, a few thousand of the Burmese soldiers had taken up arms as freedom fighters, but were labelled by the British as either rebels or dacoits. In the beginning their motives were indeed noble, but soon these roving bands found it more lucrative to rob and commit the most gruesome atrocities on their own defenceless people. It took the British authorities over four years and a force of some 60,000 soldiers and military police to bring about order in the newly acquired territories.

CHAPTER IX

THE MISSING TREASURES OF THE ROYAL FAMILY

During the evening of 28 November 1885, Prendergast was so confident that the situation was under control that it was decided to send the rest of the troops back to the transports some four miles (6.4 km) away. Left to guard the Palace for the night were the Hampshire Regiment, the 1st Madras Pioneers, and the Hazara Mountain Battery, under the command of Brigadier General White. They were ordered to occupy the outer enclosure as far as the Hlutdaw buildings and the royal Red Gate or main entrance to the inner Palace.

The *Konbaungset Chronicle* recorded that the Palace employees; maids of honour, cooks, pages, officials and attendants were only allowed to leave, and that none were to be readmitted. Totally disorientated, some remained outside the gates genuinely concerned about the fate of their King and Queen. Many cried. At this point General Prendergast made an appalling blunder:

> The Ministers asked that the palace women should be allowed to go in and out of the western gate leading to the Queen's apartments. Prendergast very naturally hesitated to grant such a concession. One of the Ministers at once naïvely suggested that the sentries might make a personal examination of everyone passing in or out! Prendergast, however, gave the required permission. How anyone in his responsible position could have been so incredibly stupid defeats the imagination.[1]

Tennyson Jesse in her novel based on these events gives the following description:

> Colonel Sladen, once a friend of Mindon Min, and himself of a royal way of doing things, was now too royal in his lavish kindness to fallen greatness. He accepted Theebaw's surrender with the provision that he should formally surrender himself to General Prendergast the following day, and then, pleased to be able to grant the request, he prevailed on General Prendergast to allow the women to go freely in and out of the West Gate. An English officer and a gentleman - damn it all! could not be harsh to the ladies. This had been the request of the Ministers – good fellows who had made no trouble and were for the most part prepared to work in with the British Government – and, after all, the Ministers were responsible for the safe delivery of the king, next day, with their lives.[2]

Tennyson Jesse was obviously at one with Lord Dufferin, who, in his assessment of Sladen had described him as a foolish, vain man. Prendergast was initially against the idea, since he felt that Thibaw might attempt to escape disguised as a woman. In this he would have been disabused by Sladen who would have told him that no Burmese male would ever adopt women's clothing, for the Burmese believed that to do such a thing would be to sap their *phon* (from the Pali *punna*: variously described as power, virtue and vital masculine energy). This would have invited universal derision and stripped him of any kingly dignity and male pride. Sladen must have been very persuasive, since the General gave his permission. The result, according to Tennyson Jesse, was that of the three hundred women employed in the Palace, by the next morning only sixteen remained, 'and the lowest women of the town, realising what a chance was theirs, streamed all night into the palace, past the English sentries, to whom all Burmese women looked alike... .'[3]

When Sladen walked into the Palace on the morning of the 29 November, he found

> even now in broad daylight, were streaming the crowds of women, field workers, big and coarse as men, fisherman's wives, harlots from the riverside, laughing and joking, bearing aloft gold cups, hanging jewellery about their necks, trampling and shouting where the delicate little Maids of Honour had fluttered, a mob let loose. [4]

This passage contains a certain amount of literary licence, since most thieves tend to conceal their spoils, lest they in turn become a victim. Why did the Ministers ask that the women have the freedom to come and go as they wished? The simple answer was so that the ladies resident in the Palace could have their dinner, since their meals were cooked outside and brought in in lacquer containers. Although General White had refused the women entry, he was told by Sladen to let them come and go as they pleased. White protested that they would loot the Palace but was assured that Sladen's words had General Prendergast's authority. It is odd, indeed, that despite the concerns of Prendergast and of White, who had warned Sladen of the consequence if the women were allowed unfettered access, on the request of one of the Ministers every person of the female sex in Mandalay was given *carte blanche* to come and go at her pleasure. It would be interesting to know who this Minister was, who apparently had so much concern for the gastric well-being of the ladies of the Palace. The name of the Taingda Mingyi springs to mind, since it was he who spent the night in the Palace with his guards to ensure that the King did not escape.

After the events of the day, Sladen retired to the Hlutdaw building where he presumably remained until awoken by the Taingda Mingyi, who said that the King and the royal party were in a state of panic. Its members probably imagined that they would now be treated in the same way that they had treated others in the past. When he proceeded into the royal apartments, Sladen found the King, Queens, and the Queen Dowager almost unattended while women of low-class were streaming in through all the western portions of the Palace. This was early in the morning. Surely, the English sentries guarding the entrances must have known or suspected that something odd was going on? While Sladen accompanied the Queens and their mother to see what was happening in their private apartments, the King collected together a large quantity of gold and bejewelled ceremonial vessels. Sladen then went to the Palace gate and called an officer and twenty-five men of the Hampshire Regiment to protect the royal family. As they passed along the vast Palace complex, he dropped sentries at each of the several royal apartments. It seems strange that Burmese official sources are totally silent as regards this disturbing event.

During the morning Thibaw and his family moved into a small summer house at the edge of the royal gardens. Sladen, having let the mob loose through the Palace during the night, now decided that as the King showed signs of fright, he might try to escape. How he could have arrived at this conclusion is impossible to understand. White

> strongly advised putting him in [the] charge of a guard at once, and a guard of the 67th Regiment was marched into the sacred confines of the palace, and had the Lord of the White Elephant [one of the King's titles] surrounded in a twinkling.[5]

Was this yet another example of spite on the part of Sladen to treat a frightened young man and four women as common felons?

After Thibaw's departure from Mandalay, General White was instructed to secure the Palace and make an inventory of the valuables that remained. He wrote to his wife, 'a great quantity of gold vessels, crown jewels, ivory and ladies wearing apparel was discovered'. And this was after the Palace had been looted, supposedly all night, by the women of the town? This leads one to wonder just how many valuable items the Palace once contained. White said that he had been disappointed in the amount and quality of jewels they had found, noting that there were only one or two beautiful pieces of French jewellery, in particular a tiara which must have cost over £1,000. Other precious items were some solid gold images of the Buddha weighing about a stone each, and some smaller ones which had lost their shape by being overlaid with gold leaf.

On 4 December 1885, *The Times of India* reported that the king's crown (court records list at least twenty crowns each used for a different ceremonial occasion) and other regalia, together with about half a million rupees in cash had now been secured. On 11 December the paper also noted that about 2.2 million rupees had been stolen from the Treasury by a Shan chief, but the man was not identified. This was one of those stories about which nothing was ever heard of again. According to the *Konbaungset Chronicle*, among the list of native officials who were present during the two days leading to Thibaw's surrender, the Sawbwa of Nyaungshwe was the only Shan chief present. The paper also recorded on 19 December that the crown jewels and much treasure had been placed in safety by Colonel Sladen. On the same day, *The Times of India* added that:

> Although the bulk of the money and other treasures in the palace are safe, there is no reason to believe that much has been stolen by the servants and attendants of the royal family....As it is a matter of universal notoriety to the force, it may be mentioned that some of the garrison obtained access to some of the buildings and rifled their contents.

This is corroborated by Pagan U Tin, who stated that British soldiers broke into the rooms where the state archives were stored in huge gilded chests and ransacked the contents looking for valuables. Much of the piles of official *parabaik* (paper) and palm-leaf records were later burnt as rubbish. (They obviously did not come within the remit of Dr Forchhammer, the professor of Oriental languages at Rangoon, who had been charged with listing the locations of valuable manuscripts in Mandalay.)

The Times of India reported that

> the greater part of the most valuable property has been preserved, the salvage including a treasure of half a million rupees belonging to the King, 30,000 rupees in two strong boxes stated to be the savings of the Queen-Mother, several of the King's crowns and much jewellery belonging to his Majesty and the Queens.

So the situation as at 19 December was that Sladen and he alone was responsible for the treasures from the Palace. Thibaw had clearly stated to Moylan, the *Times* correspondent, on 29 November that he 'had given up all the crown jewels' thereby implying that at that time the collection had not been stolen and was complete. This was confirmed by the newspaper reports that the regalia, the crowns and the King's and Queen's jewellery were safe and in Sladen's keeping.

It would appear that there were four lots of treasure in the Palace:

1. That which was under the control of the Prize Committee, and was not very valuable.
2. The regalia (168 pieces survived in the Victoria and Albert Museum, London, of which 167 were returned to Burma during 1964-65).
3. The King and Queen's personal items of cash and jewels.
4. The cash and jewels belonging to the Queen Dowager.

The last three had been put by their owners into the personal care of Sladen. It may be wondered why so many easily portable items were left with Sladen when there was no attempt on the part of the British to stop Thibaw taking anything he wanted. The reason is glaringly obvious: the King naïvely thought that his exile would be temporary and that he would be coming back.

In 1953, in a memorial to Queen Elizabeth II, the descendants of Thibaw gave another account of the events leading to the exile of the King. They claimed that Sladen had told the King and his Queens that they were being sent to Calcutta for negotiations (with the Viceroy) and that after three months they would be sent back. Earlier, in a memorial to Viceroy Lord Dufferin, dated 24 June 1886, Thibaw was still under this impression. He wrote

> that when he left Mandalay, Colonel Sladen assured him that he was only going to Calcutta for three months to discuss Burmese affairs with His Excellency the Governor-General, and that at the end of that period he would be replaced on the throne of Burma. That trusting to the well known integrity of the British Government, he gave himself up to the British officers, expecting to be sent back in a few months, and now after six or seven months had passed, and he has not yet had an interview with the representatives of the British Government.

Thibaw concluded his memorial by asking for the return of his property,

> that with reference to the list of property forwarded herewith, he states that the property was made over to Colonel Sladen to keep for him as he was afraid of losing it on the journey, and he also states that Colonel Sladen promised him that the property would be returned to him when he wanted it. He wrote some time ago and requested that the property might be sent back to him, but an answer was received that the property could not be found. He hopes that His Excellency the Governor-General will see fit to issue an order for the property to be returned.(See Appendix 1 for the list of property.)

It is interesting to note that although it was not denied that such property existed and that it had been taken into care, the subject was dismissed with the laconic comment that it could now not be found. A cursory glance at the list shows that the value of the items which 'could not be found' must have run into millions of pounds.

On receiving the memorial, the Viceroy agreed to have enquiries made about the King's property, but said that the Government could not undertake to restore these items since Thibaw had left large debts behind him. He added rather testily that the King had been allowed to retain a good deal of his property! In Burma, the Chief Commissioner instituted enquiries and wrote back to say that none of the articles on the list were with any Government officer in Mandalay, nor could any be produced. All the jewels and other portable property found in the Palace on the 30 November which was not taken by the ex-King and his fellow-deportees, was made over to the Prize Committee. Lt Colonel Budgen, the Prize Agent and Chairman of the Prize Committee, also made a statement. He noted the items which he could identify and their subsequent disposal, and also the articles that could not be identified.

Budgen mentioned that there were some items that had been sent to the Chief Engineer in Calcutta for disposal, among which were eleven so-called Buddha images of assorted sizes; these were of solid gold. These figures were in fact the ancestral images of the monarchs and chief consorts of the Konbaung dynasty which were propitiated three times a year by the reigning king and queen. These eleven items were to be kept in the Calcutta Museum as curiosities, but

Plate 63. 'A loot auction in the Palace, Mandalay' 1886.

were to be returned,

> if hereafter they should be wanted to satisfy the *bona fide* religious or superstitious desire of scions of the house of Alaungpaya, also certain items had been sent to the India Office to be put on show to the public. (See Appendix 2 for the list.)

On comparing the two lists, it is plain to see that with a very few exceptions the missing items were small and valuable.

The Dowager Queen, who was living in Tavoy with her eldest daughter (the third of Thibaws wives), also wanted the return of her property. In February 1886, scarcely three months after the King's deposition, she wrote to the Chief Commissioner with her list. In his reply, she was told that the property could not be identified, and that either it had been stolen by Burmese women on the night of 28 November 1885, or that it went to the Prize Committee. But it has been shown that the items were handed over after the looting ceased, and Sladen had put guards over the royal apartments. The items could therefore not have been stolen by the Burmese women. Lt Col Budgen in his list of 'property found in the Mandalay Palace', does not mention any of these items (See Appendix 3 for the list). The Dowager Queen then wrote to the Viceroy on 20 August 1887:

> On the morning of the 29th November 1885, Colonel (now Sir Edward) Sladen, the Chief Political Officer and party, came into the palace and said that we should have to descend to the southern gardens. The request was so sudden that I was at a loss what to do with the numerous valuable articles, my private property. Not knowing what was to become

of me and my children, I called Colonel Sladen and told him of the numerous valuable items I had in my possession. I could take away only a few, and having shown him several other articles, some made of silver and some set with diamonds in the fire-proof six-chambered vault...On this Colonel Sladen said: "The Government will not take possession of the royal family's property: they only want the King and his kingdom. Believe me, these valuable items cannot get lost: Your Highness can at pleasure take them back at any time". So saying, he personally locked the box within, then shut and locked the door and gave over charge of the vault to the Treasurer in my presence. The keys are now with me. I next pointed out to Colonel Sladen the china and glassware and rolls of cloth in the several rooms, and he then told me that if the said rooms were locked up and the keys kept with me, wherever I choose to stay, I could at any time afterwards go and take the property contained within them. These rooms were accordingly locked up... Subsequently, the items first mentioned, viz., those made of massive gold and others set with precious stones were removed to the southern Palace. There Colonel Sladen left them in charge of a man called his head Clerk and two natives of India in my presence, after having enjoined them not to mix my property with those of others. After this we went down to the southern gardens, arrangements were then made to place us on board the steamer at 3 p.m. When I expressed a wish to stay behind, Colonel Sladen replied that not only I, but even my daughter the Queen could do so and live where we pleased. I decided to stay behind accordingly, but then my children begged me to accompany them as far as Rangoon. On this I asked the Chief Political Officer whether I would be allowed to return if I were to go with them. He answered that when I got to Rangoon the Chief Commissioner would send me back comfortably; and that even if I were to go as far as Calcutta, the Viceroy would be pleased to send me back comfortably, and that I might rest assured and believe what he said for the English do not break their word. Accordingly I came down. On my arrival in Rangoon the authorities asked me to go to Tavoy and there sojourn until the country became quiet. I did not refuse, but went there and lived in the house provided by the Deputy Commissioner. My allowance, viz 450 rupees a month was found insufficient for myself, relatives and servants, and I was obliged to sell some of the few things I had brought down with me. however, I have not complained all this time. I therefore pray that the property I left behind in Mandalay may be restored to me, so that I and my relatives and servants may be able to live together in comfort.

The above, if true, sounds like Sladen at his most glib. He knew, and so in all probability did Suphayarlat and the Dowager Queen, that the women would certainly have been killed if they remained in Mandalay as ordinary citizens without day and night protection by the British. Many among the Burmese would not have forgotten that these two were the chief instigators of the massacre of the Princes, Princesses and their followers, many of whose numerous relatives would have jumped at the chance of revenge. The Dowager Queen seemed to have been asking for reassurance. She knew what she asked for was impossible, but Sladen's ready agreement that she might have it led her to believe his other claims as to the safety of her property.

When Sladen was asked to comment on her letter, he replied:

> I remember the Dowager-Queen taking me to her apartments and show-ing me three heavy well-secured boxes, which she said contained 30,000 rupees. I said the boxes would be safe but I could make no promises about the money. I received no keys whatever. I may mention that at this time, in addition to the ordinary female attendants, the Queens's apartments seemed to be full of common women, who were going about in all directions packing up bundles and carrying them away. Any separate property that the Queen-Dowager may have left after the King's abdication will have got mixed up with the other palace property and come into the hands of the Prize Committee.[6]

It is hard to believe that looting would have continued in the presence of Sladen and the Dowager Queen; the Burmese of the time were so conditioned that they would have immediately crouched down in the presence of royalty – espe-cially before someone as formidable as the Dowager. According to Hall, when Sladen was woken at daylight by the Taingda Mingyi, he immediately placed sentries in all the royal apartments. But more striking is the lack of categorical denial that these items ever existed.

The Dowager Queen, having been one of the senior Queens of Mindon would have accumulated a great quantity of jewellery. She and her daughter, Suphayarlat, had in fact added to their own collection by confiscating jewels from the other Queens, concubines and Princesses after the death of Mindon. Many of these ladies were turned out of the Palace almost destitute. A further opportunity for enrichment also came when the Princes and Princesses were massacred, and yet by the time she had got to Tavoy and sold off a few items, she was poor enough to qualify for a pension from the British Government.

There was also the curious case of the Nga Mauk ruby ring which was said to be a stone of 98 carats and was reputedly 'without price'. The Pauk-myo-sar, who was the Shwetaik Atwinwun (Treasurer) informed British officials that he had been present when this gem together with jewellery and other valuables had been handed over to Sladen in the presence of Nicholas and the Taingda Mingyi. The Treasurer had made out an incomplete list of these articles on a *parabaik* and this was given to Nicholas together with the articles, and handed over to a guard under an English officer. That there was such a list is authenticate by an account in the *Konbaungset Chronicle*, which stated that at about noon Sladen arrived and Thibaw told him that as he was concerned about the safety of the crown jewels and other valuables, he would like to see that they were in safe hands. The Treasurer then handed over to Sladen a list of the collection. Yet

Sladen was to deny the existence of such a list.

On 6 September 1965 the following letter appeared in *The Times*:

> Sir, Allow me, as the senior grandson of King Thibaw – the last Bur-
> mese King – to convey to the people and Government of Britain,
> through the columns of your esteemed paper, the appreciation of the
> grandchildren of King Thibaw in Britain's magnanimous gesture in
> returning to Burma our ancestors regalia.

(Earlier, *The Times* had reported on 11 November 1964 that 167 items, known
as the Mandalay regalia, and conserved in the Victoria and Albert Museum, had
been handed to General Ne Win, the then Burmese head of state.)

> For the information of the British public may I add that besides the
> famous 'Nga Mauk' Ruby, once known, I believe, as the 'Chrismore
> Ruby' in the United Kingdom, my grandfather H.H. King Thibaw,
> handed over to the British Army officer, on that fateful day (29 No-
> vember, 1885), seven other precious ruby rings of the same category
> as the Nga Mauk ruby, and also his (the King) and Queen's personal
> jewels...May I appeal to the good and righteous sense of the British
> public as well as the British Government to endeavour their best to
> trace and return to Burma the missing items of the Burmese King's
> regalia and their personal effects which seem to be spread around your
> countryside as souvenirs of the Conquest.....Taw Phaya.

Back in 1886, the Viceroy and Lady Dufferin had visited the Mandalay Palace
and were taken to inspect the 'prize'. She later commented: 'Very poor prize it
is! Thibaw's ladies were much too sharp for our soldiers, and managed to walk
off with everything.'[7] It is hard to reconcile her remarks for it would appear that
the reverse was true. However, the following account from the *Saturday Evening
Journal* of August1886, contradicts the so-called 'poor prize' description:

> The Burmah regalia: – I hear that prices realized at the recent sale of
> the Burmese regalia were more than satisfactory to all concerned, with
> the exception, perhaps, of certain native purchasers. For beauty, value
> and rarity combined offered irresistible attractions to Marwaree [Indian
> traders and money lenders] cupidity; and so keen was the competition
> that more than one sable Streeter [the London firm who valued and
> sold some of the jewels] of Burra Bazaar was a victim of the unpleasant
> experience known in commerce as "burning one's fingers". But the
> most precious possesion of the deposed monarch came into Messrs
> Hamiliton's hands too late to admit of their including it in the catalogue.
> It consists of a pair of brilliant solitaires, which have been worn on
> state occasions by four successive Kings of Burmah. These veritable
> "gems of purest ray serene" are exquisitely cut, and weigh 15 carats.
> Their history which is amply authenticated, should add largely to their
> great intrinsic value.

It will come as no surprise to learn that these items were not on the list of Lt
Col Budgen, the Prize Agent and Chairman of the Prize Committee. On 11
November 1886, Sladen was asked if he could help in the search for the lost

rubies and the *parabaik* list which gave details of the other jewellery. His private papers in the India Office Library and Records show that he drafted three replies. In the final version dated 25 February 1887 he wrote that although he recalled seeing the Atwinwun in the Palace that morning he did not remember seeing any *parabaik*. Indeed, he was convinced that due to the turmoil in the Palace, it would have been impossible to have produced even an incomplete list. However, the list had been drawn up the previous evening, and there was ample time to note these items.

Sladen was also unable to recall the name of the officer with whom he entrusted the valuables, but he felt sure that the man 'did his duty to the best of his ability'. He admitted that no one was in charge of the property in the Palace and that items were being carried away before his eyes. Sladen stated that he asked for a guard to be put on the royal apartments to prevent further looting. He seemed to feel that this was a matter for congratulation. In the draft of 22 January 1887, Sladen admitted

> I am afraid the above facts are not of a very enlightening character. If they do not assist your efforts to trace the missing property, they may convince you that it is due to prompt action at the time that we got possession of any portion of the crown regalia. Had I been an hour or two later in entering the palace that morning, the whole of it must have gone. As it is, we have secured more than a mere remnant.

Sladen added that what ever items came his way were handed over to the Prize Committee of which he was not a member.

There is, however, a curious note in Sladens papers where he had written a list of 'loot' taken by him at the capture of Mandalay. This included such items as 'Queen's writing desk (French)', and a 'large state chair' which was intended for the Viceroy. Sladen wrote:

> Almost all were got on the first day of the surrender and were either taken from palace women who were bolting with them – or from some of my followers who had recovered them from other looters...I do not want them and will gladly make them over to the Prize Agents.[8]

It is unclear whether he had brought these items back to England, but it does contradict his claim to have handed over everything to the Prize Committee. Also the thought of Burmese peasant women making off with French writing desks and large state chairs seems a little incongruous.

Unusually, nothing appears to have been written about the contents of the Shwetaik (Treasury building) which was in a separate part of the Palace complex. This would have been securely locked and could not have been forced open by the women. The King had silver, ruby, jade and amber mines, and there must have been numerous items made of these materials. Also the taxes, which were paid in cash and precious metals, and the large collection of gold objects which were part of the regalia, had been housed there. Regarding the eleven solid gold statuettes which had been sent to the Chief Engineer in Calcutta, Harvey, in his *History of Burma* mentions that there were between thirteen and seventeen, and that they varied in height from six inches to two feet (15-63 cm). According to him, they were sent by the Prize Committee to the Superintendent, Governor's Estate, Bengal and where, as he casually comments 'as there was nobody to take any interest in them, they were ultimately melted down'.[9] No mention was made of a collection of ten Hindu gods made of gold and silver, and which ranged in height from six to eighteen inches (15-46 cm). The collection was kept in the Hmannan (Glass Palace) where they were worshipped by the king and queen. It would appear that the Palace was awash with valuables despite the depredations of the so-called Palace ladies. To begin with were the items which were found in the Palace, and those which Thibaw took with him. Then there were those which he, his Queen and the Dowager Queen claimed were there. A large number of objects were sold at public auctions in the Mandalay Palace and by jewellers in Calcutta, Hong Kong and London. According to Woodman, 'the finest jewels were sent to Queen Victoria'.

As wild rumours spread of the fabulous treasures from the Mandalay Palace, the merchants were not idle. Seeing the possibility for a quick profit, they began importing imitation rubies from Europe into Burma and then exporting them as genuine Burmese rubies. Prospective purchasers were warned of this practice in the *Times of India* of 13 February 1886.

Sladen was to recall that large and small utensils of gold, studded with precious stones lay in heaps on the floor of the verandah of the huge audience chamber. It is not surprising therefore that the British soldiers helped themselves.

On 14 April 1894, the *Illustrated London News* published the following:

The Hidden Treasure at Mandalay

Burma Public interest has been directed to the almost forgotten subject of Burma by the sensational story of the alleged theft of a large portion of the royal treasure by British soldiers. The dying confession of a private of the West Surrey Regiment that he and a comrade, Private William White, had made away with a portion of the regalia is startling enough, but has not taken the authorities so much by surprise as might have been expected. [Sir Steuart Bayley, the Secretary to the Political Department at the India Office, is quoted in *The Times*, of 2 April 1886 as stating that 'the Burmese Crown and jewels certainly were missing'.] All who were engaged in the campaign of 1885 knew that an immense quantity of valuables had been abstracted from the Palace either before or after the British occupation. At the time suspicion largely rested on the Burman Ministers and maids of honour, and every effort was made to trace the jewels without avail. Now we hear of them after a lapse of nine years through a death-bed confession. From particulars given by a correspondent who was with General Prendergast's force, and who entered the Palace with the troops, it appears that the keenest interest is being shown by the Indian Government in the matter, and the result of Private White's journey to Burma, where he has gone to recover the treasures is anxiously awaited.

As regards the regalia, which was valued surprisingly at only £21,191 and 10 shillings, on 13 October 1886 *The Times of India* stated that

from King Theebaw's palace at Mandalay a magnificent collection of jewellery and plate has been sent to England by the Viceroy and has been lent to the [Colonial and Indian] Exhibition by the Secretary of State for India. There are gold vases of different sizes, dishes of quaint shapes (some in the form of a duck), betel boxes, reliquaries to hold the teeth of Buddha or other objects of veneration, jade ornaments, daggers and swords, dresses, hats, slippers, a State umbrella, and most noteworthy of all - drinking cups with large cone shaped covers which envelope the vessel, a gold bottle with a crayfish shaped head, and King Theebaw's horoscope written on palm leaves. Most of these articles are heavily set with diamonds, rubies, emeralds, sapphires, pearls, and other precious stones. The collection has been placed in cases adjacent to the Ceylon Court.

Just what treasures the Mandalay Palace contained will now never be known.

Chapter X

The leading Players in the Mandalay Drama

As to some of the leading characters in this last drama of the Konbaung dynasty, Thibaw, ex-Lord of Life and Death from the 'golden' city of Yadanabon (The Mound of Jewels), ended his days at wind-swept dreary Ratnagiri (The Jewelled Mountain). *The Times of India* was there to report the arrival of the ex-king at his final place of exile. It noted that he was a strongly built middle-sized man, with a round fair Chinese complexion, and that he wore a slight moustache. His appearance, gait and behaviour was that of a refined person. He was smartly dressed in his national costume, and 'on each side of his breast there were attached to the silk coat, two rows of diamonds and rubies of the size of small chestnuts in gold setting, which shone brightly in the morning rays of the sun'. His two Queens were equally splendid and blazed with jewels. Suphayarlat wore a 'huge diamond necklace some three or four rows deep, while a sort of coronet, set with rubies, emeralds, and diamonds was fixed into the folds of her hair just above her forehead'. She was observed to be wearing English shoes, unusual for someone who supposedly detested anything Western.

Long empty years of exile lay ahead for Thibaw. Squabbles within the family and with a series of Political Officers in charge of him were to be his lot. To add to his troubles, his eldest daughter became pregnant by one of the Indians employed to guard him. This was a terrible scandal which shocked his ex-subjects back home, for the Burmans have always considered Indians as inferiors. In the early 1900s, groups of Burmese headed by some of his ex-officials and accompanied by leading dancers and musicians, were occasionally allowed to visit the exiles. Photographs exist of a sad-looking Thibaw holding an audience surrounded by melancholy men in their now defunct court robes. He never left his residence in thirty years. Bored, without means of distraction, and suffering from depression and heart problems he died at the age of fifty-eight on 15 December1916. He was survived by Suphayarlat and their four daughters.

The junior Queen, her sister, had died in 1912 and her body had been sealed in a metal coffin. When Thibaw passed away, his body, too, was treated in the same way. Burmese royalty were not buried but were either cremated or entombed. For whatever reason (possibly astrological) this entombment was not performed until 19 March 1919. But before this could take place, the Government required the coffins to be opened in the presence of witnesses to certify that the bodies were there. In Thibaw's case in its entirety, since it was feared that if the body or even part of it were to be taken to Burma, it might become a focus for those advocating independence for the country.

Fortunately, due to the representations of the ex-Queen and her daughters to the Viceroy, the Lt Governor of Burma, Sir Reginald Craddock, and the Governor of Bombay, Thibaw was spared this last indignity, and he was finally entombed with his junior wife at Ratnagiri. Suphayarlat, that wilful and obstinate woman who was the cause of so much unhappiness to her people and the loss of her country, was allowed to return to Burma on 18 April 1919. She saw out her last days complaining of penury. Although given an adequate pension, she tended to behave rather grandly, spending large amounts on the Buddhist clergy, with the result that she was always in debt. This was her way of attempting to atone for her past cruelties not only to her half brothers and sisters, many of whom were mercilessly butchered, but also to the innumerable courtiers who suffered at her hands when she ruled in Mandalay.

It must be pointed out that even in old age, and her glory days well and truly over, Suphayarlat was an extremely difficult woman, and behaved as if she was still in power. She would not allow anyone to approach her unless they were prepared to crawl on their hands and knees; a form of court etiquette which was practiced in most South-East Asian countries. The surprising thing was that this was something she expected of Burmans and foreigners alike. Understandably, Rangoon society, at the apex of which were the ever-so-grand and powerful English *burra memsahibs*, avoided her. Even the educated Burmese upper classes had nothing to do with her, for it was well known that she had a tendency to borrow money which was never repaid. Besides, by the 1920s this 'exotic' creature from another age was totally out of place in the modern city. Although it was claimed that she was stunningly beautiful in her youth, those who saw her now were astonished at her rapid descent into a hideous old age.

Just before her death, the following extract was published in *The Times* of 12 February 1925, from its Rangoon correspondent:

> The Rangoon Gazette, is commenting on the report of a Committee of the General Council of the Burmese Association on the alleged grievances of the Burmese ex-Queen Suphayarlat, says that the Committee was appointed for the purpose of embarrassing the Government, and argues that no good purpose can be served by such a manoeuvre through the newspapers agree that any real grievances, if they exist, should be removed. The Committe appointed consisted of U Tok Kyi, of the Indian Legislative Assembly, U Ma Thein, of the Burma Legislative Council and U Ba Hlaing, editor of *New Burma*. Their report is a long one, but the main features are:- That Suphayarlat was accommodated in an old rickety building, ill kept and ill furnished and quite unsuited to the dignity of the Royal Consort of the last King of Burma. That a member of the Civil Service instead of a Deputy Superintendent of the Police should be in attendance on the ex-Queen. That the pension of 2,500 rupees (£166) a month is insufficient to keep

Suphayarlat out of debt, and is less than half the pension granted to her when she was exiled in Ratnagiri. That at Ratnagiri, the ex-Queen was provided with two motor-cars and three landaus, but in Rangoon she is provided with no conveyance at all. That the ex-Queen had been deprived of her landed properties, which when Queen of Burma, she held in her own right. That she has not been given the historic jewels which were handed to Colonel Sladen on the cap-ture of Mandalay, one of which, the Nga Mauk, is said to be worth a kingdom. That the remains of King Thibaw and the second Queen should be brought from Ratnagiri and laid to rest by the side of their Royal father King Mindon Min at Mandalay. Finally, the Committee strongly recommended the Nationalist Party to make represen-tations to the Government in order that the ex-Queen may receive treatment befitting her dignified position as ex-Queen of Burma.

Plate 64. The Kin Wun Mingyi.

Yet the 'concerned' authors of this article did not lift a finger to alleviate her plight.

Nevertheless, when Suphayarlat died in 1925 she was given an impressive funeral by the Burmese before her entombment on Pagoda Road. Strange to say, the dilemmas faced by the country's ex-royals were ignored by successive Burmese governments after independence in 1948, and Suphayarlat's tomb lay damaged and neglected until well into the early 1970s.

The Kin Wun Mingyi, the only wise and competent minister in Thibaw's government, died in 1908 at the ripe old age of eighty-six. In his early days, he had been a monk, but had left the order at the request of King Mindon who appointed him as a minor official. He was a diligent man, and worked his way through the civil service posts and at the time of Mindon's death was Prime Minister, Foreign Secretary and Commander-in Chief of the army. He was un-doubtedly loyal to his royal masters and when asked, gave honest advice. But since many of his suggestions were not ones which Thibaw and his overbearing Queen wanted to hear, he rapidly lost influence to the notorious and pushy

Taingda Mingyi who became the court favourite.

On one occasion, when the Kin Wun Mingyi's advice had displeased Thibaw, Suphayarlat turned on him viciously and told him that he was behaving like an old woman, and suggested that he put on a *htamein* (female skirt). She duly sent him a set of women's clothes. In Burma this was the ultimate insult to a male, especially to someone of his standing and age. However, when war with the British was imminent the frantic King and Queen swiftly recalled him from obscurity. He gallantly took part in the peace negotiations and the settlement of the kingdom. In 1887, he was honoured on the occasion of the Queen Victoria's Jubilee by being made a Companion of the Most Exalted Order of the Star of India in the audience hall of the Mandalay Palace. Later that year, he was awarded a pension of 1,000 rupees a month. Unfortunately, because of his close association with the Raj, some modern-day Burmese so-called historians have branded him a traitor, and have held him responsible for the annexation.

Plate 65. The Taingda Mingyi.

There appears to be no taint attached to him concerning the disappearance of the royal jewels. He seems to have been an honest civil servant, or if not completely honest, then at least more so than many of his compatriots. According to Sir Herbert Thirkell White, the Lieut Governor of Burma, he was, 'a man of high character, incapable of any base or treacherous act. His personal record was unimpeachable, and he lived and died in honourable disregard of wealth.'[1]

If the Kinwun Mingyi represented reason and light, Taingda Mingyi, that 'partner in crime' of Suphayarlat, was darkness and evil personified. He had literally got away with murder; indeed many murders. The irony of his situation could not have been lost on him when he was asked by the British to head the Hlutdaw under the chairmanship of none other than Colonel Sladen. During his days of power, it was widely known that he had organized gangs of dacoits roaming the countryside; in return for his protection they supplied him with half the loot. Thibaw once asked why these robber bands were so difficult to apprehend. One daring official wittily replied that it was because when royal troops were sent, these bands simply disappeared behind a *taing* (the word meaning a pillar and the prefix of the minister's title), and as a result could not be caught.

On hearing of his appointment by Sladen, public outrage was predictable. *The Times of India* wrote on 21 December, 1885:

> The Kin Wun Mingyi has apparently been shipped off and the Taingda allowed to remain. Whether this was by accident or design has not yet clearly transpired. If it is a mistake it is a most unfortunate one, and if it is by design it is difficult to understand what could have prompted Colonel Sladen to such a course. Both these men are probably at heart equally opposed to English rule, because it strikes at the roots of the arbitrary power they have hitherto wielded. But the Kin Wun Mingyi is a man of some ability, who had always tried to keep Thibaw back from his wilder excesses, and who did his best to induce him to accede to the British demands and to avoid a perfectly hopeless war. The Taingda, on the other, is simply an utterly brutal and blood-thirsty ruffian. It was his zeal as a butcher in the massacre of the Princes that brought him into favour, and he has retained the King's confidence by a consistent display of the same spirit ever since. It is notorious that, though a Minister of the Burmese Crown, he was in league with bands of dacoits. He was the foremost of the war-party, loudly declaring that he would drive the English into the sea. After receipt of the ultimatum, he had urged the King to kill all the Europeans remaining in the country, and when war broke out, he undertook to bring the heads of Colonel Sladen and General Prendergast to the King. Of all the ruffians who made up the recent Burmese Government, the Taingda is the worst, yet Colonel Sladen has associated himself with him in the present temporary government of the country, while the comparatively respectable Kin Wun Mingyi is sent into exile. When the news of this condonation of the Taingda's brutalities and his employment by Colonel Sladen reached Rangoon, it was received with absolute incredulity. Now, however, it is put beyond any reasonable doubt, and the Chamber of Commerce has given expression to the popular opinion on the subject by protesting against the employment of of such a 'blood stained ruffian' as 'a blot on the good name of the British nation' and 'a bad omen to the people of Upper Burma of what they may expect under British rule', a man of his antecedents would not be employed in any civilized country as a hangman, and it is impossible to describe the feeling of disgust and dismay that the news has excited among the Europeans in Rangoon.

It is difficult to reconcile the above with Sladen's thoughts that the Minister 'was somewhat the victim of prejudice', and was happy to work with him in governing the country. But Bernard, the Chief Commissioner, thought otherwise and arrested the Taingda on 25 December 1885, against Sladen's

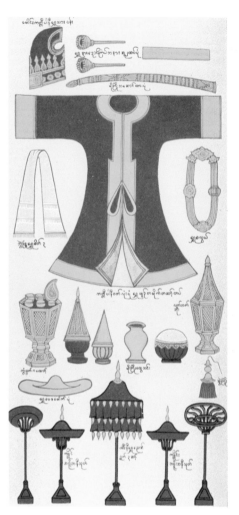

State military uniform, regalia and saddlecloths applicable to the Thado rank granted to Maha Bandula in 1852. Parabaik painting based on a 19th century manuscript. (See Chapter IV.)

State Robes and regalia applicable to the Thado rank granted to Maha Bandula in 1852. Painting based on a 19th century manuscript. (See Chapter IV.)

Plates 66 and 67.

Plate 68 (above, left). The Lion Throne and Konbaung regalia, Mandalay Palace.

Plate 69 (left). Burman generals and officials. *Circa* 1870s.

Plate 70 (above). The summer house in which King Thibaw surrendered to General Prendergast in November 1885, Mandalay Palace gardens.

Plate 71. The young King Thibaw and Queen Suphayarlat standing ominously by an empty throne (1885).

Plates 72 and 73. Parts of the gold regalia of the Konbaung dynasty looted by the British in 1885 and restored to Burma in 1964. Paintings based on a 19th century manuscript.

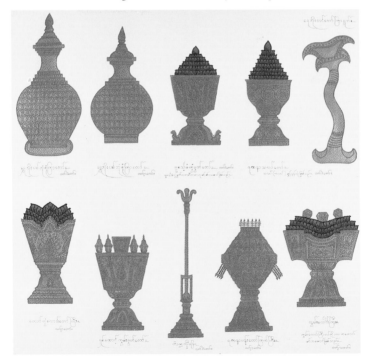

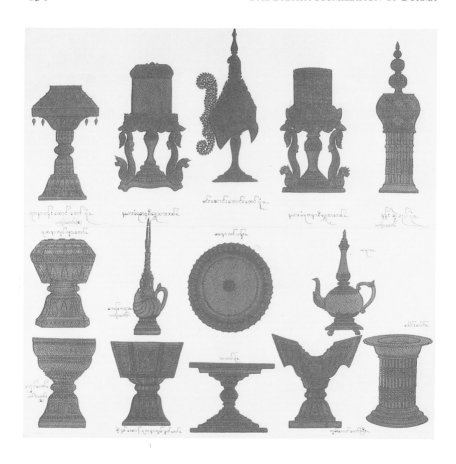

Parts of the gold regalia of the Konbaung dynasty looted by the British in 1885 and restored to Burma in 1964. Paintings based on a 19th century manuscript.

Plate 74 (above); 75 (right, top); and 76 (right, bottom).

အခါတော်ဝင်ရာသီပုံတော် ၊

ရုပ်ချစ်ကြာပေါင်းကြီး (ဇယ်ဖြစ်)
စစ်ကိုင်းမြို့ တန်ဆောင်းမင်း (မင်းတုန်း) အလယ်ပစ်ပါး
ရုပ်ချိုတုရှာ‌ခေါင်ကြီး (ပြည်ဖြို့)
ပစ်ဝင်တော်ပြု ရုပ် မင်းတရားကြီး (မင်းဥ) ပစ်ပါး
ရုပ်သိန္ဓေ ‌ခေါင်ကြီး (ဖိုးဖျ)
အဆေ ၊ ပြုရုပ် တန်ဒ် မင်း (မင်းကွန်း) ဂုံ မင်း
ရုပ်ချစ်ပ ချာ‌ခေါင်ကြီး (မင်းဝ်ဖာဖ)
ရုပ်ဒ်(ဖဖ) ချိုဒ်ဖုဖုချ (မင်းဒ်ဖျ)
ဒ်ဖန္ဒ ‌မင်း (ဉ ‌ခေါင်တ်)
ဖိုးဖ ‌ဒ် ‌ခု‌ခ (မင်း‌တော်ဖျ ‌ခုကြ)
ဒ်ဖန္ဒ်ဖ ‌မင်း ‌ဖ‌ဖချ ‌ဖျဖ‌ဖာ‌ဖ ‌ချ‌ဖော့‌ဖ‌ဖာ‌ဖ‌ဖ
ဖေ‌ဖ‌ဖ ‌ဖ‌ဖာ‌ဖ ‌ဖ‌ဖ‌ဖ‌ဖော‌ဖ‌ဖ
ဒ်ဖ ‌ဖ‌ဖ‌ဖ ‌ဖ‌ဖ‌ဖ‌ဖော‌ဖ‌ဖ‌ဖ‌ဖ‌ဖ
ဒ်ဖ ‌ဖ ‌ဖ‌ဖ ‌ဖ‌ဖ
ဒ်ဖ‌ဖ‌ဖ ‌ဖ‌ဖ‌ဖ‌ဖ‌ဖ ‌ဖ‌ဖ‌ဖ (‌ဖ‌ဖ‌ဖ‌ဖ‌ဖ‌ဖ‌ဖ)

ရတနာ ပြိ ဉ် ကုန်း ‌တာင်‌ရွှေ‌ပြည် ‌ကြီ ကုတ်တုပ် အဆောင်းမင်း
‌တ‌ပုင်ကြီ‌ရ‌ဖက် တုတော် ပုံ့ အရုပ်တော် ‌ဖု
‌ဖ ‌ဖဖ ‌ဖဖ ‌ဖ‌ဖ ‌ဖ‌ဖ ‌ဖ ‌ဖ။

‌ဖ‌ဖ‌ဖ‌ဖ‌ဖ‌ဖ‌ဖ‌ဖ‌ဖ‌ဖ‌ဖ‌ဖ‌ဖ‌ဖ‌ဖ
‌ဖ‌ဖ‌ဖ‌ဖ‌ဖ‌ဖ‌ဖ‌ဖ‌ဖ‌ဖ‌ဖ‌ဖ ‌ဖ‌ဖ
‌ဖ‌ဖ‌ဖ‌ဖ ‌ဖ‌ဖ ‌ဖ‌ဖ ‌ဖ‌ဖ ။

‌ဖ‌ဖ‌ဖ‌ဖ‌ဖ‌ဖ‌ဖ‌ဖ‌ဖ‌ဖ‌ဖ‌ဖ‌ဖ‌ဖ‌ဖ‌ဖ‌ဖ
‌ဖ‌ဖ‌ဖ‌ဖ‌ဖ‌ဖ‌ဖ‌ဖ‌ဖ‌ဖ‌ဖ‌ဖ‌ဖ‌ဖ‌ဖ

‌ဖ‌ဖ‌ဖ‌ဖ‌ဖ‌ဖ‌ဖ‌ဖ‌ဖ‌ဖ‌ဖ‌ဖ‌ဖ‌ဖ‌ဖ‌ဖ
‌ဖ‌ဖ‌ဖ‌ဖ‌ဖ‌ဖ‌ဖ‌ဖ‌ဖ‌ဖ‌ဖ‌ဖ‌ဖ

wishes, and sent him to Calcutta. This course of action prompted his nephew and grandson, ex-members of the Hlutdaw, to defect to the Myinzaing Prince who had taken up arms against the British. *The Pioneer*, on 26 April 1886 wrote: 'It would seem that Colonel Hooper [Provost Marshal of Mandalay] had every reason to doubt the loyalty of certain members of the Hlutdaw.' In early 1886 the Taingda had a meeting in Calcutta with Lord Dufferin, who thought him 'an intelligent old man' and told him that until Upper Burma was pacified, he would be treated as a guest and then returned to Mandalay! According to Sir Herbert Thirkell White, the Taingda was detained for several years before being

Plate 78. 'Engagement with dacoits at Chinbyit, Upper Burma' (1887).

sent back to Burma with an allowance. He died a poor man in 1896, having lost his wealth in foolish speculations. Did this man know too much?

Regarding some of the leading British players, when Lord Dufferin's term of office came to an end in 1888 he returned to London and was created a Marquis by Queen Victoria. The name of Ava, the old capital of Burma was added to his title. He then pursued a diplomatic career as he had done before his Viceroyalty, and died in 1902.

General Prendergast should have been set for a glittering end to his military career, as the Government of India wanted him to take sole command in Burma. Although it asked the British Government for a special dispensation to allow for this, it was not approved. The powers-that-be were influenced by an error of judgement that Prendergast had made earlier. Without going into detail,

Plate 77 (left). The ten solid gold ancestral images of the rulers of the Konbaung dynasty and their consorts melted down by the British. Paintings based on a 19th century manuscript.

suffice it to say that a Colonel Hooper, the Provost Marshal at Mandalay, in early January 1886 had photographed dacoits as they were being executed by firing squad. Moylan, the correspondent of *The Times* and no lover of the military, played this distasteful story for all it was worth. Following the furore, questions were asked in the House, and the readers of *The Times* thought the cat o'nine tails and the treadmill too good for this officer. Lord Dufferin told Prendergast to attend to the matter, if necessary with the utmost severity. Prendergast, however, merely reprimanded Colonel Hooper. From that point he was sidelined to various adminstrative positions, all with grand names but none requiring his military skills. He died on 24 July 1913.

Edward Bosc Sladen was born at Madras on 20 November 1827. He was the son of Dr Ramsey Sladen of the East India Company's service. After being sent home to be educated at Oswestry School in Shropshire, Sladen gained an East India cadetship, and on his return to India in 1850 was commissioned as a second lieutenant in the 1st Madras Fusiliers. He served in the second Anglo-Burmese war under General Godwin, and was present at the relief of Pegu in December 1852 and the second investment in January 1853. Sladen was gazetted Lieutenant on 1 February 1853 and appointed an assistant commissioner in Tenasserim. He obviously demonstrated outstanding abilities to the authorities since this was a very rapid promotion.

In 1856-7, he took part in the operations against the insurgent attacks by the Shans and Karens, during which he was severely wounded. In February 1858 he rejoined his regiment which was engaged in suppressing the Indian Mutiny, and was present at the capture of Lucknow in March 1858. When his regiment returned to Madras he was again deputed to work in Burma. He joined the Indian Staff Corps at the time when the Madras Fusiliers became a Queen's Regiment. He was gazetted Captain in June 1860; Major in 1869; Lieutenant Colonel in 1875. In 1866 he went to Mandalay as the Agent of the Chief Commissioner, and there he was responsible for obtaining a commercial agreement with King Mindon. Sladen travelled extensively in the remoter part of the country and was able to obtain much valuable information on on the prospects for trade with China from the various tribes he met.

He was promoted Commissioner of Arakan in 1876, and remained there until 1885 when he was appointed Chief Political Officer to the Burma Field Force. He was knighted for his services on 26 November 1886, and retired from the service on 14 April 1887. Sladen died at the age of sixty-three in London on 4 January 1890, a bare three years after his retirement.

That he was not well regarded in government circles is shown by a letter from Lord Dufferin to the Secretary of State for India, in which he wrote:

It is better, I think, that he should go home, he has done excellent

service and displayed considerable courage, and undoubtedly we are in-
debted to him for the capture of
the king, and, to a certain degree, for there having been no
fighting in Mandalay. I will,
therefore, venture to suggest
that he be made a Knight.
A K.C.S.I. [A Knight Com-
mander of the Star of
India] would be too much
I think. He is a foolish and
vain man, and, I imagine,
he was not quite loyal to
Bernard [the Chief Com-
missioner]. No one was a
stronger annexationist, but
his notion was to set up the
Hlutdaw and to govern
through it, with himself as
President. The plan was an
impossible one, and, I believe, it was self interest which
induced him to urge it.[2]

On the other hand, *The Illustrated
London News* of 16 January 1886 had
nothing but praise for him:

Plate 79. Colonel Sladen, British Commissioner at Mandalay.

Colonel E. B. Sladen, who accompanied General Prendergast at Man-
dalay, has for some years past held the appointment of Commissioner
of the British province of Arracan. From long residence in that country, and from his five years experience as political agent at the Court of
Mandalay. Colonel Sladen is undoubtedly one of the best authorities
on Burmese affairs; and he has for some years past strongly advocated
its annexation by the British Government of India. Colonel Sladen will
be remembered as the leader of the successful expedition to discover
the old trade routes to Western China by way of Bhamo, in 1868. He
received from King Min-don-Ming the Burmese order of the highest rank
with a decoration of twelve chains [a *salwe*].

That Britain stole the kingdom of Burma is surely self evident; from the first
conquest of Arakan and Tenasserim, which might under the imperialist notions
of the time have been thought to be the legitimate spoils of the victor, to the
annexation of Pegu, for which there can be no justification whatsoever. And
finally, the seizure of the remaining territory in the interest of commerce. Many
of the traders and merchants became rich as a result of Burma being drawn
into the British Empire. They were, however, outraged when the British Gov-

ernment decided that the Indian Government should levy an income tax to pay for the war and the subsequent pacification.

Entrepreneurs moved into the Burma oilfields, teak extraction increased, the gem and metal mines were worked, and the Bombay Burma Trading Corporation and the Irrawaddy Flotilla Company were able to pay excellent dividends to their shareholders. At the time Burma was called the Rice Bowl of Asia, so great was its production, and trade in this staple was mostly in the hands of British merchants. There was a thriving import and export business, and Burma was on the tourist map. The merchants and their accomplices the missionaries had achieved their heart's desire, which was free trade.

But there still remains the question of the fate of parts of the regalia and the royal jewels, much if not most of which is still missing. Portable and valuable items were no doubt stolen by the maids of honour and other attendants. Others items were obviously taken by the women of the town and some British soldiers. All this while the Taingda Mingyi guarded an apprehensive young man and his family.

It stretches the imagination that the Taingda could have been unaware of what was going on, since his guards were all Burmese who would have obeyed him without question. If he absented himself for a while to indulge in a little thievery on his own behalf there was no one to stop him. He knew precisely where the state treasures were stored. But even he would only have been able to take such items as he could carry about his person. Some pieces were probably stolen by the Taingda's guard, who after rousing Colonel Sladen, took the opportunity to melt away into the night. If Private William White's story in *The Illustrated London News* is to be believed, he and his companion appear to have taken a portion of the regalia and buried it. According to the report, it would seem that White obtained immunity from prosecution and was promised a commission on any of the regalia that might be discovered with his assistance.

At the time the report appeared, the ex-soldier was earning fifty shillings a week working on an extension to the London docks. Why was he never heard of again? Why were the jewels never seen on the market? There were many dealers in precious stones in both Rangoon and Mandalay, all of whom would have known that anything that they were offered by an Englishman who did not appear 'pukka' must have been obtained illicitly. Therefore they could be bought at a fraction of the value, broken down and sold piecemeal. It seems that White's story was either a pure fabrication or, possibly that he and his comrade had hidden a few pieces but that he was reluctant to share what little he had secreted away with anyone else.

As to the fate of the personal jewellery of the royal family, all the evidence seems to point to Colonel Sladen as the prime suspect, as was the view of the

King, the Queen and the Queen Dowager. It is nowhere stated that these items did not exist. It has always been claimed that they could not now be found, or that they had been made over to the Prize Committee, the records of which give the lie to this claim.

In the case of the King's jewels, there were four witnesses to the hand-over of this property. These were the officer who was to guard them and who subsequently could not be identified by Sladen; Nicholas, Sladen's chief clerk; the Taingda Mingyi; and the Shwetaik Atwinwun who drew up a list which he gave to Nicholas. After the deposition of Thibaw, and with the Taingda Mingyi in Calcutta for a number of years, it would have been a simple matter to ask him to verify the Shwetaik Atwinwun's statement. Was Nicholas questioned, or was it not necessary? Did the Viceroy have his own suspicions?

At the time, it was of course unthinkable that a British officer and a gentleman could be responsible for such a crime. After all, it was certainly not the sort of thing which could be allowed to become public knowledge, as the effect on the Empire would be catastrophic. Besides, it would have undermined the entire British administration throughout the world. If this were the case, it would explain a number of things, such as why Sladen retired at the comparatively early age of sixty, and received the KCB, the lowest order of knighthood. His protestations of innocence were accepted without question, and the complainants were told that there was no evidence that Sladen had taken charge of any property on behalf of the ex-King.

The official view was that all the property which the ex-King had not taken with him had been handed over to the Prize Committee. Then why did the Shwetaik Atwinwun say that he had given Sladen a list of the property, quoting three other witnesses, whom he must have believed would corroborate his claim? This official had nothing to gain by lying and indeed much to lose. Had the Indian Government thought him a perjurer, it would hardly have given him a pension of 500 rupees a month, which it did in August 1887.

Why did Sladen choose the Taingda Mingyi to sit as the senior Burmese representative in the Hlutdaw, and allow the Kin Wun Mingyi to leave Mandalay? Sladen, above all people, must have been aware of the Taingda's responsibility in the slaughter of the royal kinsmen and the murder of the followers of the Princes in exile. Sladen must have known how his actions would have been viewed by the British in Burma, and indeed by the Burmese in Mandalay who despised the Taingda. Why did Sladen refuse to arrest him, a task which had to be carried out by Bernard who sent him to Calcutta, where his treatment was to say the very least unusual? Why was the man who *The Times of India* described as not fit to be a common hangman in any civilized country, treated by the Government of India as a guest?

What of the officer who commanded the guard over Thibaw's property? How many officers were on duty at the time? It is known that only the Hampshire Regiment under General White was guarding the Palace gates; the remainder of the force was on the boats over four miles away. It should not have been too difficult to find this officer. And what of Nicholas, who remains just a name? Any evidence that he could have given would have been crucial.

If Sladen did take the jewels, what became of them? The only confirmation available is information on the 'Nga Mauk Ruby', described by the grandson of Thibaw to have been also known as the 'Chrismore Ruby' in the United Kingdom. So that item at least, was stolen and sold in Britain. If Sladen was the perpetrator, did he perhaps have to share with others and split the treasure four or five ways? Or was Sladen innocent as he claimed?

After more than a hundred years it is mere speculation as to what really happened to the jewels and parts of the regalia. It is possible that hitherto unavailable Burmese records may supply further clues. On the other hand, maybe it is too late for any further investigation. Pending additional research, readers must reach their own conclusion based on the evidence provided.

CHAPTER XI

SELECTIONS FROM INDIAN INDIGENOUS OPINION

The First Anglo-Burmese War, 1824-6

As to the opinion of the average Indian concerning the first Anglo-Burmese war, most of India would scarcely have known of it, or cared greatly if it did. One must assume that the sepoys of the Company's army were indifferent, as long as they were paid and due attention given to their religious observances. This seems to have extended to allowing them to destroy or deface as many of the Buddhist images they could find, as to them one enemy was much like another. If they were literate (and most were not) there was one Bengali newspaper which they might have read, the *Samachar Darpan*, first published in 1818. But it was hardly likely to have been controversial, published as it was by three missionaries. The next vernacular newspaper was the *Bombay Samachar*, which began publication in 1830 and was printed in Gujerati.

British newsletters had been circulating from the sixteenth century onwards. The first British newspaper, the *Bengal Gazette*, (better known as *Hickey's Gazette* or *Journal* after the name of its founder, J.A. Hickey) was published in Calcutta in 1780. This was a scurrilous organ and ceased publication within about a year. By the time of the first Anglo-Burmese war there were a number of English newspapers, including the *Indian Gazette*, founded in 1783 and merged with the *Bengal Hurkaru* in 1833, and the *John Bull of the East*. But surprisingly, these papers appear not to have had their own corr espondents. The course of the war was charted by letters from the officers either to the newspapers or to friends with their permission to have them published, and of course the commanders' despatches.

The Second Anglo-Burmese War, 1852-3

Criticism of the second war came mainly from the British papers, both at home and in India, and was concerned not with the justice of the war but with its conduct. On the 22 November 1852, *The Bombay Gazette* remarked: 'The intelligence from Rangoon is, as usual, unsatisfactory,' and goes on to recommend to its readers an article in *The Times* which delt with the conduct of the war with 'withering sarcasm' and undeniable accuracy, castigating both the military and naval commanders.

On the 24 March 1853, the *Friend of India* commented on General Godwin and his desire to march to Ava, because he detested the navy and resented his reliance on it. He said that if Ava was to be attacked, it should be done in the proper way, by troops marching there, as had been done by General Campbell in 1826, and not sailing on boats. The paper commented,

> he appears unable to get beyond the idea that every thing done or
> omitted to be done by General Campbell ought to be done or omitted
> to be done by General Godwin.

On 23 June 1853 the *Bombay Gazette* published excerpts from the *Burma War Blue Book*, which showed a division between Sir John Littler, the Military Member of the Viceroy's Council, and Lord Dalhousie. Sir John wanted to 'strike at the heart of the enemy to bring the war to an honourable conclusion, or a conclusion at all', whereas Dalhousie was content with Pegu. This according to his critics was only putting off the inevitable third war.

The Third Anglo-Burmese War, 1885.

The third war proved to be a rich seam for native criticism since the phony reasons for the war were only too apparent.

The Hindu, 22 November 1885:

> Is India to be fleeced, asks *The Hindu*, everytime that the expansion of
> Brtish commercial interest pushes itself on new ground? Would England
> have dared to proclaim war against Russia in the manner in which she
> has been threatening Burmah for the past few days? In dealing with
> that power, England pretended to pay strict regard to the principles of
> international morality and resented every apparent disregard of them
> on the part of Russia. But Burmah is a weak state, and India can be
> forced to pay with less appearance of injustice. So England resolves to
> undertake a war in a quite reckless and wanton spirit. We hope that
> better counsels will prevail yet and the immediate cause of the war –
> the alleged wrong to the Bombay Burma Trading Corporation – will
> be settled by arbitration.

The Times of India, 9 November 1885:

> The vernacular papers do not seem to approve of the intended expedi-
> tion to Upper Burmah. *The Bombay Chronicle* seriously warns the Gov-
> ernment against engaging in what it regards as a 'costly, destructive war
> with a neighbouring power merely because a British mercantile corpo-
> ration, trading with Burmah and dealing with its native monarch for its
> own gains, has managed to come to a misunderstanding or disagree-
> ment with that monarch in respect of its private business transactions.
> The affair is purely one of private commercial dealing between the
> Bombay Burmah Trading Corporation and King Thibaw, and there is
> nothing in it as yet known to make it the cause of a justifiable war
> between British India and the State of Burmah....They are certainly
> welcome to do all that may be deemed necessary for the just protection
> of British national interests in Burmah and the maintenance of British
> prestige and political supremacy. But anything beyond that, anything
> done to make a mere private disagreement between two parties, one in
> India and one in Burmah the cause of a war between British India and
> Native Burmah, would hardly be capable of defence?

The Rast Goftar, 9 November 1885

This paper cordially approves of the action of Mr. Bright in condemn-
ing the war preparations and says the Government have been led up to
their bellicose attitude by the intrigues of merchants and speculators
in Rangoon. They have for a long time been casting longing eyes upon
the rich and fertile territory of Upper Burmah out of pure self-interest.
There is not the shadow of a pretext for waging war against a weak
state and a gentle people, now that the French Government have given
their assurance that they have no desire whatever to enter into any
negotiations with Thibaw that would be prejudicial to British interests.
Supposing for a moment that the Bombay Burmah Trading Corporation's version of their dispute with Thibaw is correct, could that be a
sufficient reason for the English Government launching into a 'great
war' with the Burmese?

The Bengalee, 11 November 1885

The traditions of England are the traditions of freedom. She has ever
been the friend of the weak and the helpless; and now in persuance of
a policy of selfish aggrandizement, she does not hesitate to destroy the
liberties of a weak and defenceless people. It will not do now to say
that Thibaw is despotic and cruel and that in the interests of humanity
it is necessary to depose him. If Thibaw has been cruel, his cruelties
have long since been condoned by the British Government. England
now goes to war, not on behalf of suffering humanity, not at the call
of an oppressed people, but to create a new market for British goods;
and the infamy of the transaction is enhanced by the hypocritical excuse
which is being put forward viz., that the Government has undertaken
to avenge the interests of an injured company.

The Dainik, 21 November 1885

The line of commerce of the English is the cause of this complica-
tion. They entered India as merchants, and within this one hundred
and fifty years they have established an extensive dominion. Again they
have entered Burmah as merchants and are about to ruin that country.
An independent king has a right to govern in his own way. We cannot
understand why others should oppose him. If his behaviour does not
suit you why go to his country?

The Indian Mirror, 21 November 1885

War against Upper Burmah has been declared against the strongest
remonstrances of the whole native population expressed through the
Native Press with a unanimity of opinion which we have never wit-
nessed before. And never was native opinion disregarded with such
open unmistakable marks of contempt.

The Muslim Herald, 8 December 1885

Had a quarrel as the one which has terminated fatally to Upper Burmah,
ever taken place between two European powers, small or great, it would
probably have been referred to a mixed arbitration court and decided
according to the principles of International Law; but Burmah is in the
far East and could not claim such a right. The King's first and second

proclamations breathe a spirit of friendliness and submission that would disarm any incensed powerful neighbouring potentate of his anger and move him to pity; but where material gain is the test of all friendship, even the most trifling quarrel assumes the magnitude of a nation's dishonour and the result can easily be guessed. Where the necessities of trade are a ruling element in the machinery of government, even the considerations of policy have often to give way.

The Burdwan Sanjibani, 31 December 1885

The Rangoon Chamber of Commerce says in its memorial to the Viceroy praying for the annexation of Burmah, that it will be cruel to place the Burmese again under a native king, as they are willing to be under British rule. The memorial states that new markets are indispensably necessary for the sale of British goods. The English merchants pray for the opening of a new market at the cost of the independence of Burmah. How Christian these merchants are.

The Samachar Chandrika, 31 December 1885

The merchants of Rangoon are advising the annexation of Burmah. Their suggestions ought not to be acted on. Every line in the memorial of these English merchants is full of selfishness. The Government will suffer very much if it listens to such suggestions.

The Bengalee, 7 January 1886

In announcing the annexation of Burmah, we deplore the decision of the Government. It is something worse than a crime – it is a blunder of the gravest magnitude. The Burmese have now ceased to be a nation; and England the august mother of free nations has made them so! We have not the heart to write about the subject. We fear the honour of England has been compromised beyond redemption before the eyes of Asia.

The Indian Mirror, 20 January 1886.

The proclamation by which the annexation of Upper Burmah to the British Empire is declared is unique for the terms in which it has been drawn up. In other similar cases, the Government of India always assigned some reason or show of reason for such a stretch of power, as is involved in the act of absorbing the territory of some neighbouring or allied state. It is either the misrule of the reigning dynasty or the hostility of a neighbouring people that is put forward as a ground for superseding the established government in the state....It might have been more to the point if it had been stated that it was to satisfy the demands of the commercial and manufacturing interests in England, and open out new markets for English trade in the regions bordering on Upper Burmah that this act, so distasteful to the people of a neighbouring state [India] has been committed.

The Indian Spectator, 1 March 1886

So the House of Commons has thrown the entire cost of the Burmah expedition on the shoulders of the Indian taxpayers. It is very kind of the Honourable House, and kinder still of the Ministers. Are they not all honourable men?

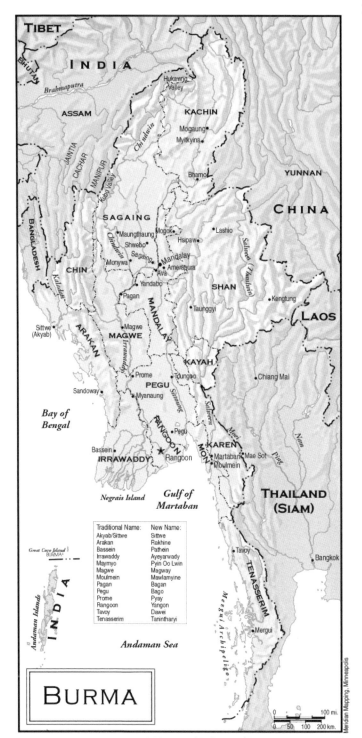

Map 2. Topographical map of Burma.

Notes

Chapter II

1. Andrea Correa, in Fitch, *England's Pioneer to India*, p. 132.
2. Factory record: Misc., p.55. India Office Library and Records.
3. Hakluyt Society, series 11, vol. LXVI, p. 45.
4. Woodman, *The Making of Burma*, p. 26.
5. ibid., p. 26.
6. ibid., p. 28.
7. Phayre, *History of Burma*, p. 221.
8. Symes, *An Account of an Embassy to the Kingdom of Ava*.
9. Phayre, *History of Burma*, p. 221.
10. Bayfield, *Historical Review of the Political Relations between the British Government and the Empire of Ava...to the end of the year 1834.*
11. *Bengal Secret and Political Consultations*, 29 April 1802, No. 23.
12. ibid.
13. ibid., No. 20.
14. ibid.
15. ibid., 2 September 1802, No. 9.
16. ibid., 29 May 1810.
17. ibid.
18. Woodman, *The Making of Burma*, p. 54.
19. Phayre, *History of Burma*, p. 223.
20. ibid., p. 225.
21. ibid., p. 226.
22. Harvey, *History of Burma*, p. 283.

Chapter III

1. Hall, *Europe and Burma*, p. 113.
2. Snodgrass, *The Burmese War*, p. 8.
3. Htin Aung, *A History of Burma*, p. 213.
4. Bruce, *The Burma Wars*, p. 88.
5. Phayre, *History of Burma*, pp. 244-5.
6. Pearn, *History of Rangoon*, p. 120.
7. *Konbaungset Chronicle*, p. 386.
8. *Government Gazette*, 17 March 1825.
9. Pearn, *History of Rangoon*, p. 125.
10. Woodman, *The Making of Burma*, p. 93.
11. ibid., p. 112.
12. Htin Aung, *The Stricken Peacock*, p. 32.
13. Htin Aung, *A History of Burma*, p. 213.
14. Hall, *Europe and Burma*, p. 124.

15. Indian Political Consultations. Range 194, Vol. 5, Consultation 15, 6 February 1836.
16. Indian Political Consultations. Range 194, Vol. 15.
17. Woodman, *The Making of Burma*, p. 111.
18. Burney's letter, 12 July 1837, India Secret Consultations, vol. 8.
19. Burney's letter, Rangoon, 12 July 1837, Indian Secret Consultations, Vol. 8.
20. Col Benson's letter, 18 July 1838, Indian Secret Consultations, 22 August 1838.
21. Pearn, *History of Rangoon*, p. 139.

Chapter IV

1. Ferrand, *Relations de voyages* ..., p. 10.
2. Shwebo Mi Mi Gyi, *Maha lu-ye-chun* ..., p. 17.
3. *The House of Commons Debate*, 17 June 1850.
4. Minute by the Governor-General, Lord Dalhousie, 12 January 1852, India Secret Consultations, vol. 173, no. 38.
5. Sann Thamein, *Myanmar-thway* ..., pp. na.19-na.20.
6. Papers relating to hostilities with Burma (1852). C.1940.
7. Papers relating to hostilities with Burma (1852). C.1940.
8. Minute by the Governor General, 22 January 1852, in Woodman, *The Making of Burma*, p. 540.
9. Baird (ed.), *The Private Letters of the Marquess of Dalhousie*, pp. 188-910.
10. Papers Relating to Hostilities with Burmah (1852), C.1490, pp. 39-40.
11. Laurie, *The Second Burmese War*, .p. 28.
12. Bruce, *The Burma Wars 1824-1886*, p. 136-7.
13. Papers Relating to Hostilities with Burmah (1852), C.1490, pp. 39-40.
14. ibid., p. 14.
15. Minute by the Governor-General, 22 Janaury 1852, in Woodman, *The Making of Burma*, p. 540.
16. ibid., p. 542.
17. Papers Relating to Hostilities with Burma (1852). C.1940.
18. The Governor-General's reply to the Commodore's statement, in Woodman, *The Making of Burma*, p. 546-7.
19. Minute by the Governor-General, 12 February 1852, p. 138.
20. Papers Relating to the Hostuilities with Burmah (1852), c.1490, p. 75.
21. ibid., p. 67.
22. Cobden, *How wars are got up in India: The Origins of the Burmese War*, cited by Woodman, *The Making of Burma*, p. 145.
23. Pearn, *History of Rangoon*, p. 172.
24. Baird, *Private Letters of the Marquess of Dalhousie*, p. 246.
25. ibid., pp. 260-61.
26. ibid., p. 369.
27. ibid., p. 262.
28. ibid., p. 359.
29. ibid., p. 228.

30. ibid., p. 229.
31. Hall, *Dalhousie-Phayre Correspondence 1852-56*, p. 3, fn. 3.

Chapter V

1. Dalhousie-Phayre Correspondence, Letter 23.
2. Dalhousie-Phayre Correspondence, Letter 26.
3. India Secret Consultations, vol. 4 1893, Consultation no. 19, 30 September 30 1853.
4. Woodman, *The Making of Burma*, p. 175.
5. 'Journey of Lt. Sconce and Capt. Watson onto the Shan States in 1863-4' *Journal of the Burmese Research Society*, 14, 3, 1924.
6. Htin Aung, *The Stricken Peacock*, p. 60.
7. ibid., p. 61.
8. ibid., p. 61.
9. Lawrence Letters, India Office Library, Eur. Mss. F.90, 10 December 1866.
10. Htin Aung, *The Stricken Peacock*, p. 62.
11. 'Burma and the American State Papers' (Christain), *Journal of the Burmese Research Society*, vol. 26, pt.2.
12. Woodman, *The Making of Burma*, p. 195.
13. India Foreign Department Proceedings, vol. 769, 1873.
14. Woodman, *The Making of Burma*, p. 159-60.

Chapter VI

1. Aitcheson-Mackenzie Wallace, Dufferin Papers, 22 October 1885.
2. Hall, *Europe and Burma*, p. 169.
3. Correspondence relating to Burmah since accession of King Thibaw, October 1878, C.4614 (1886).
4. Pearn, *History of Rangoon*, p. 250.
5. Woodman, *The Making of Burma*, p. 220.
6. Lyall, *The Life of the Marquis of Dufferin and Ava*.

Chapter VII

1. Woodman, *The Making of Burma*, p. 223.
2. Pearn, *History of Rangoon*, p. 250.
3. Home Correspondence, 1886, vol. 85.
4. Pearn, *History of Rangoon*, p. 252.
5. Correspondence relating to Burmah since accession of King Thibaw, October 1878. C.4614, (1886)
6. Correspondence relating to Burmah since accession of King Thibaw, October 1878. C.4614, (1886).
7. Home Correspondence, 1885, vol. 80.
8. Scott, *Burma from the Earliest Times to the Present Day*, pp. 320-1.
9. Correspondence relating to Burmah since accession of King Theebaw,

October 1878, C. 4614, 1886, pp. 225-6.
10. Marquis of Dufferin and Ava microfilm reels 516-534, India Office Library.

Chapter VIII

1. Stewart, *The Pagoda War,* p. 74.
2. Sladen to Duran, Secretary to the Government of India. Burma, Further correspondence relating to Burma, no. 3 (1886). C4887.
3. Military Proceedings, November 26th, 1885; Prendergast-Dufferin, 29 November 1885, Dufferin Papers.
4. Burma, Further Correspondence Relating to Burma, no. 3 (1886), C.4887.
5. Woodman, *The Making of Burma,* p. 245.

Chapter IX

1. Hall, *Europe and Burma,* pp. 180-1.
2. Tennyson Jesse, *The Lacquer Lady,* p. 320.
3. loc. cit.
4. ibid., p. 321.
5. General White-Mrs White, December 7th, 1885, White Papers.
6. Indian Foreign Department Proceedings, October 1887; Section E, no. 178. Note by Sladen. 6.3.1886. in Desai, *Deposed King Thibaw of Burma in India, 1885-1916,* pp. 41-2.
7. Dufferin, *Our Viceregal Life in India,* p. 187.
8. Papers of Sir Edward Bose Sladen, India office Library and Records, EUR.E.290/79m.
9. Harvey, *History of Burma,* pp. 327-8.

Chapter X

1. White, *A Civil Servant in Burma,* p. 147.
2. Dufferin Papers, Lord Dufferin to Kimberley, 21 March 1886.

APPENDICIES

APPENDIX 1. LIST OF PALACE PROPERTY PREPARED BY THE SHWETAIK ATWINWUN, 28.11.1885.

List of property prepared by the Shwetaik Atwinwun (Treasurer) on the eighth evening of the month of Tazaungmon of the year 1247 (28 November 1885) and handed over to Colonel Sladen by Thibaw and his Queen. This is corroborated by the *Konbaungset Chronicle* (Burmese titles for the objects have been amended to give their correct reading]. The signature of H. Fanshawe, the Political Officer, appeared at the bottom of the list.

Utensils:
* Four solid gold betel boxes
* One spittoon set with diamonds, rubies and emeralds.
* One wash-hand basin set with diamonds, rubies and emeralds.

Personal ornaments:
* Four *salwe* (solid gold chains of rank worn by the king) set with jewels.
* Thirteen pairs of nadaung (earrings) set with large diamonds.
* Three pairs of ruby and three of emerald earrings.
* Seventeen *lair-swair* (necklaces) set with diamonds.

Let-sut-daw (rings):
Among the rings were twenty-one set with rows of diamonds; the celebrated Nga Mauk ruby ring. The *Konbaungset Chronicle* stated that this ruby entered the royal collection at Inn Wa in 1661, during the reign of Pye Min (r.1661-72) of the Nyaungyan dynasty. A man named Nga Mauk who lived at a village called Chindwin presented the ruby to the King; the weight of the ruby was ninety carats. (On 8 October 1991, an article by Sithu Aung in the *Loke-thar-pyu-thu* [Working People's Daily] said that after the signing of a commercial treaty by the Kin Wun Mingyi and Charles De Remusat, the Foreign Secretary, in Paris in 1873, a French mission arrived at Mandalay. One of its aims was to obtain a licence to work the ruby mines at Mogok and Kyatpyin. When shown the Nga Mauk by Mindon and asked to value it, the gemmologist was unable to do so. The King then told the French that if they were unable to appraise this specimen it was beyond his comprehension how they could evaluate the quality of the rubies they hoped to extract and pay him the appropriate amount. He therefore refused permission. The French did not give up and tried several times. In March 1885, a request for a licence was submitted to Thibaw by M. Bonvillein, assistant to M. Haas, the French Counsul. An outright gift of 100,000 rupees

together with 1,200,000 rupees to cover a period of four years was offered. But the British learnt of the matter through a spy in the palace. The Nga Mauk, which was said to have been 'priceless' or 'worth a kingdom' only weighed 90 carats. The article reported that a ruby weighing 500 carats had recently been found).

* Seven ruby rings known respectively by the names Kyen Keyagyee, Hlawka-tin-galay. According to the above chronicle, this ruby was brought to the Court at Amarapura during the reign of Badon Min (r. 1782-1819) carried in a *hlaw-gar* warboat, hence its name 'the-little-ruby-which-was-carried-in-a-warboat'. Its weight was about twenty carats. The other rings were Auyoonme, Anee-gyi (the large red), Kyakkyoukkyes, Thayet Khaw, San Kyouk (or the 'example' ruby - for some reason it was held up as an example. Its weight was six carats.

* Five ruby rings, not identified. The chronicle, however, offers three names and 'and other valuable rubies which were included in the list [given to Sladen]'. These were:

* The Hlaw-gar-tin-gyi. This ruby, too, was brought to court in a *hlaw-gar* warboat in the month of Waso in 1837, during the reign of Sagaing Min (r. 1819-37). It was presented by Thiri-zeya-yaza who was the Kathe-so-thugyi or headman over a community of Manipuris at Kyatpyin, Mogok. It was found at Tha-phan-pin Kyauk-twin-taw (royal ruby mine) and carried to the capital in a gilded warboat, hence its name. It weighed over forty carats.

* The Sin-ma-daw (royal female elephant) ruby. This ruby weighed ten carats. It was carried on the back of a female elephant from the royal stables.

* The Naga-bo (dragon chief).

The king's *Du-yin-daw* (robe of state) and accessories:
The king's robe of state was decorated with the nine auspicious jewels. There were also two *baung* (official headdresses) with ornaments of diamonds, emeralds and rubies, and three *thar-myee-yat* (flywhisks) with gold handles set with rubies.

The chief queen's *Mair-li-kar-tan-sar* (celestial robe) and accessories:
This state robe was embellished wth diamonds, emeralds, rubies and pearls. Her state jewels consisted of five flower-shaped head ornaments set with diamonds, one of which had two large emeralds; two gold combs with diamonds; four diamond pendants; one loose emerald; one gold bracelet and belt set with diamonds; one pair of diamond earrings; twenty-four necklaces each made up of 120 pearls; and one stand and two crests also set with diamonds.

Other objects of solid gold:
Betel eating paraphernalia of solid gold consisting of one large *hintha* (duck)

shaped betel box with ruby eyes, and seven small *hton-bu* (lime boxes used in preparing betel) set with diamonds; one large cone-shaped gold vessel set with rubies (cover for a drinking water goblet of gold); three gold boxes; one large salver with stand and two large basins all of pure gold; one large *mya-pa-khet* (or emerald cradle, made entirely of gold and set with emeralds and rubies (for the royal children); and one large sofa of solid gold.

Items of silver were thirty large silver *phalar* (bowls); one chest containing silver ingots and betel boxes; four chests with ornaments of silver; and a chest with 100,000 kyat (rupees).

Trappings for the animals used on state occasions:
Four sets each of elaborate accoutrements for the state elephants and horses. These were of gold cloth set with rubies.

Dah-daw (swords of state):
Seven swords with scabbards and handles of gold set with diamonds and rubies.

Clothing and materials:
Twenty-one large boxes containing jackets, *pasoes* (elaborately woven sarongs worn by males), silk handkerchiefs and silk materials.

APPENDIX 2. LIST OF PALACE PROPERTY PREPARED BY LT COL W.T. BUDGEN, 6.10.1886

On 6 October 1886 [almost a year later] Lt Col W. T. Budgen, who was the Prize Agent at Mandalay, commented on the property discovered in the Palace. He said that he could not identify many of the objects which appeared in the above list. Nevertheless, he listed those that had come into his possession. According to Budgen's list, selected pieces from the crown property were dispatched either to England, the Mint Master in Calcutta or sold to Messrs Hamilton & Co.

Objects sent to England:
Of the 'fabulous' ruby rings listed, he felt that those he saw were of poor quality, except for a 'snake ring' and another with nine rubies, together with a gold stand set with jewels.
* The King's bejewelled state robe and belt, five jewelled crowns and two flywhisks with gold and ruby handles.
* Two large emeralds
* Solid gold salver with rubies.
* Three gold cone-shaped covers set with diamonds and rubies (only one in

the Shwetaik Atwinwun's list).
* Six jewelled *dahs* (swords). (The Shwetaik Atwinwun listed seven swords.)
* He said that there were only two gold betel boxes but many gold stands, one of which was sent to England.

Items which were either sent to the Mint Master in Calcutta or sold by Messers Hamilton & Co., included:

* An undisclosed number of gold stands.
* Two very large solid gold basins sent to the Mint and acquired by Hamilton & Co.
* 'Many' boxes and vessels of gold.
* Numerous chests containing betel boxes and silver ingots, boxes, bowls and cups of silver.
* Silver *kyat* (rupees) amounting to about 1 1/3 lakhs (130.000) from various parts of the palace.
* Many chests of clothing, native silks and other materials.

Budgen denied seeing any jewelled accoutrements for the state elephants and horses; failed to mention the solid gold ancestral images which according to Harvey were melted down at the Mint; and failed to list the numerous objects sold in Mandalay by Truda & Co., and in Hong Kong.

A breakdown was given by the IFDP (Indian Foreign Department Proceedings, National Archives of New Delhi and Bombay Archives [unpublished]) in 1886 [Sec-E; No.288]

Of the total amount (in Rupees) received from the sale of what was termed Prize Property:	Rs.477,705
It said that the money discovered in the Palace amounted to:	136,169
Sale of objects held in the palace [presumably to officers and government officials]:	20,869
The better quality items were sold by Truda & Co., Mandalay:	87,450
Jewellery and gold artifacts sold by Hamilton & Co., Calcutta:	67,963
The Calcutta Mint received silver items:	43,144
Gold items:	122,107
	Rs.955,407

At the time there were roughly Rs.10 to the pound sterling. (The total would be worth nearly sixty times as much today, according to *The Daily Telegraph*, London, 11 June 1999.)

APPENDIX 3. LIST OF PALACE PROPERTY PREPARED BY THE DOWAGER QUEEN, 20.8.1887

On 20 August 1887, a letter together with a list of personal property was presented to the Viceroy of India by Sinbyumashin, the Dowager Queen. She stated that at the annexation these articles were stored in the *taik* (brick building) within the *puegon* (building complex) west of the northern doorway (of the Palace platform).

(a) The contents of a leather trunk:
* Ten pairs of *nadaung* (tube-like earrings) with diamonds and one with rubies.
* Seven diamond necklaces.
* One string of diamonds cut in the *kha-ye-thi* fruit (*Mimusops elengi*) pattern.
* One gold watch and chain with diamonds.
* One small gold *kyok* (spherical box).
* Three pairs of solid gold *chay-guin* (anklets) with diamonds: two in the *naga* (dragon pattern).
* One large bowl and two spittons of solid gold.
* Two picture frames set with brilliants, and one album of photographs.
* One small casket set with diamonds containing a portrait of [Edward] the Prince of Wales.

(b) The contents of a teak box:
* One necklace with large diamonds.
* One gold comb in a peacock design set with diamonds.
* One bag with silver pieces.

(c) The contents of a metal safe:
* Five bags of pure silver pieces.
* One bag of 10,000 one *mu* (*anna* - equivalent to 1/8 of a rupee) silver pieces.
* Twenty gold watches and chains set with diamonds.

(d) Silver *kyats* (rupees) totalling 30,000 in a teak box.

(e) Objects of solid silver:
* Nine silver bowls weighing 150 ticals each.
* Nine silver bowls weighing 100 ticals each.
* Two salvers, one stove, two fire tongs, two curry saucepans, one pot for cooking rice and one kettle.

Another list of articles was presented by Sinbyumashin, the Queen Dowager on 20 August 1887. All the items listed, which were of solid gold (with the weight of each appended), were consigned to Colonel Sladen by the Dowager on the morning of 29 November 1885. (IFDP October; 1887; Sec-E; No. 177.)

[1 viss = 3.61 lbs or 1.596kg, there are 100 ticals to the viss].
Solid gold objects:
* Boxes set with jewels:
* Two boxes each weighting 1 viss [1.6kg]
* Four oval boxes each weighing 50 ticals [800g]

Solid gold objects:
* Solid gold salvers with stands:
* Salver with *chinthe* (lion) shaped stand weighing 1 viss [1.6kg]
* Salver on dragon stand: 1 viss [1.6kg]
* Salver set with green glass: 1 viss [1.6kg]
* A *Naga* (dragon) shaped salver used as drinking cup: 70 ticals [1.12kg]
* Two *kyar* (lotus) shaped salvers: 50 ticals [800g] and 40 ticals [640g]
* Two salvers set with green glass: 40 ticals [640g each]

Other items of solid gold:
* Two *htway-in* (spittoons) set with jewels.
* Two conical covers: 1 viss (1.6kg)
* Two wash bowls weighing 60 ticals (960 g) and 10 ticals [160g]
* One wash stand (for the face): 50 ticals [800g]
* Another for the hands: 60 ticals [960g]
* Turban stand with cover and saucer: 1 viss [1.6kg]
* Tray with three legs and cover: 50 ticals [800g]

Cooking utensils of solid gold:
* Pot for cooking rice: 15 ticals [240g]
* Eight bowls for curry: 70 ticals [1.12kg each]
* Nine saucers: 45 ticals [720g each]
* Cup with long handle for drinking water: 15 ticals [240g]

BIBLIOGRAPHY

General Works

Abbott, Gerry, *The Traveller's History of Burma*, Bangkok (Orchid Press), 1998.

Alexander, J. E., *Travels from India to England*, London (Parbury, Allen & Co.), 1827.

Allott, Anna, *The End of The First Anglo-Burmese War*, Bangkok (Chulalongkorn University Press), 1994.

Anon, 'Mindon's Heirs', *The Nation*, Supplement, Sunday 26 August 1862, Rangoon.

Baird, J. A., *Life and Letters of the Marquess of Dalhousie*, London (William Blackwood and Son), 1910.

Bayfield, G. T., *Historical Review of the Political Relations between the British Government in India and the Empire of Ava...to the end of the year 1834*, Revised by Lieut. Col. Burney, British Resident, Calcutta (Baptist Missionary Press), 1835.

British Burma Gazetteer, Rangoon (Government Press), 1880.

Bruce, George, *The Burma Wars 1824-1886*, Hart-Davis, London (MacGibbon), 1973.

Cox, Capt. Hiram, *Journal of a Residence in the Burmhan Empire*, London (John Warren), 1821.

Crawfurd, J., *Journal of an Embassy from the Governor-General of India to the Court of Ava, in the Year 1827*, London (Henry Colburn), 1829.

Crosthwaite, Sir Charles E., *The Pacification of Burma*, London (Edward Arnold), 1912.

Dalrymple, A., *Reprint from Dalrymple's Oriental Repertory, 1791-7 of Portions Relating to Burma*, Rangoon (Published by Authority), 1926.

Dautremer, J., *Burma Under British Rule*, London (T. Fisher Unwin), 1913.

Desai, N. S., *History of the British Residency in Burma 1826-1840*, Rangoon (University of Rangoon), 1939.

____, 'Queen Me Nu and her Family at Palangon' *Journal of the Burma Research Society*, XIX, ii, 1929.

____, 'The Rebellion of Prince Tharrawaddy and the Deposition of Bagyidaw King of Burma, 1837' *Journal of the Burma Research Society*, XXV, iii, 1935.

____, 'Bagyidaw as Ex-King, 1837-1846' *Journal of the Burma Research Society*, XXVIII, iii, 1938.

____, *Deposed King Thibaw of Burma in India, 1885-1916*, Bombay (Bharatiya Vidya Bharan), 1967.

Dufferin, Lady Hariot, *Our Viceregal Life in India; Selections from my Journal 1884-1888*, London (John Murray), 1890.

Fennand, G., *Relations de voyages et de textes geographiques arabes, persans, et tures relatifs a l'extreme orient du VIIIe au XVIIIe siecles*. Paris (Laroux), 1913.

Foucar, E. C.V., *Mandalay the Golden*, London (Dennis Dobson), 1963.

Fyche, Albert, *Burma Past and Present*, London (Kegan Paul), 1878.

Gait, Sir Edward, *A History of Assam*, Calcutta (Thacker, Spink & Co.), 1926.

Gouger, Henry, *Personal Narrative of Two Years' Imprisonment in Burmah*, London

(John Murray), 1860.

Grant, Colesworthy, *Rough Pencillings of a rough Trip to Rangoon in 1846*, Calcutta 1853, repr. Bangkok (Orchid Press), 1995.

Hall, D. G. E., *Dalhousie-Phayre Correspondence 1852-56*, London (Oxford University Press), 1932.

____, *Europe and Burma*, Oxford (Oxford University Press), 1945.

____, *Burma*, London (Hutchinson's University Library), 1950.

____, *A History of South-East Asia*, London (Macmillan & Co Ltd), 1955.

Harvey, G. E., *History of Burma from the Earliest Times to 10 March 1824, the Beginning of the English Conquest*, London (Longman Green & Co.), 1925.

Horton Ryley, J., *Ralph Fitch: England's Pioneer to India and Burma*, London (T. Fisher Unwin), 1899.

H.R.H. The Fourth Princess, *Private Affairs*, printed privately, 1931.

Htin Aung, Mg., *The Stricken Peacock, Anglo-Burmese Relations 1752-1948*, The Hague (Martinus Nijhoff), 1965.

Htin Aung, Mg., *A History of Burma*, London (Columbia University Press), 1967.

Kyan, Daw, 'King Mindon's Councillors' *Journal of the Burma Research Society*, XLIV, i, 1961.

Kyan, Daw, 'Prizes of War 1885' *Researches in Burmese History*, (Department of Historical Research, Rangoon), 3, 1979.

Laurie, W. F. B., *Our Burmese Wars*, London (Allen), 1880.

Lloyd, Christopher, *Captain Marryat and the Old Navy*, London (Longmans Green & Co.), 1939.

Lyall, Sir Alfred, *The Life of the Marquis of Dufferin and Ava*, London (John Murray, vols I and II, 1905.

Maung Maung, *Burma in the Family of Nations*, Amsterdam (Djambatan Ltd), 1956.

Moore, Joseph, *Eighteen Views Taken at and near Rangoon*, London (Thos. Clay), 1825.

Myint, Ni Ni, Daw, *Burma's Struggle Against British Imperialism (1885-1895)*, Rangoon (The Universities Press), 1983.

Nisbet, John, *Burma Under British Rule and Before*, London (Archibald Constable Ltd), 1901.

Pearn, B. R., 'King Bering's Campaigns' *Journal of the Burma Research Society*, XXIII,1933.

Pearn, B. R., *History of Rangoon*, Rangoon (American Baptist Mission Press), 1939.

Pemberton, Capt. R. Boileau, *Report on the Eastern Frontier of British India*, Gauhati (Department of Historical and Antiquarian Studies in Assam), 1966.

Sangermano, Vincentius, *The Burmese Empire a Hundred Years Ago*. 1838, 1883, repr. Bangkok (Orchid Press), 1995.

Sarkar, S. C., 'The Negrais Settlement and After' *Journal of the Burma Research Society*, XX, ii, 1932.

Scott, Sir J. G., *Burma from the Earliest Times to the Present Day*, London (T. Fisher Unwin Ltd), 1924.

Scott O'Connor, V. C., *Mandalay and Other Cities of the Past in Burma*, London (Hutchinson & Co.), 1907.

Singer, Noel F., 'Royal Ancestral Images of Myanmar' *Arts of Asia*, May-June, 1994.

____, 'Maha Bandoola The Younger' *Arts of Asia*, November- December 1994.

____, *Old Rangoon; City of the Shwedagon*, Gartmore, Scotland (Kiscadale Publications), 1995.

Snodgrass, J. J., *Narrative of the Burmese War*. London (John Murray), 1827.

Stewart, A. T. Q., *The Pagoda War*, Newton Abbot (Victorian [& Modern History] Book Club), 1974.

Stuart, J., *Burma through the centuries*, London (Kegan Paul, Trench, Trubner), 2nd ed., 1910.

Symes, Michael, *An Account of an Embassy to the Kingdom of Ava sent by the Governor-General of India in the Year 1795*. 3 vols. London (The Oriental Press), 1800. Repr. Bangkok (Orchid Press), 2000.

____, *Journal of his Second Embassy to the Court of Ava in 1802*, London (George Allen & Unwin Ltd), 1955. Repr. Bangkok (Orchid Press), 2000.

Tennyson Jesse, F., *The Lacquer Lady*. London (William Heinemann), 1929.

____, *The Story of Burma*, London (Macmillan), 1946.

Than Htun, Dr, ed., *The Royal Orders of Burma, AD 1596-1885*, Kyoto (Centre for Southeast Asian Studies, Kyoto University), Pts. I-X, 1983-90.

Trant, T. A., *Two Years in Ava from May 1824 to May 1826, by an officer on the staff of the Quarter Masters' Department*, London (John Murray), 1827.

White, Sir Herbert Thirkell, *A Civil Servant in Burma*, London (Edward Arnold), 1913.

Woodman, Dorothy, *The Making of Burma*, (The Cresset Press), 1963.

Yi Yi, Dr, 'A Note on King Mindon's Administration' *Bulletin of the Burma Historical Commission*, Rangoon, 1, 11, 1960.

Yule, Captain Henry, *Narrative of a Mission sent by the Governor-General of India to the Court of Ava in 1855*, London (Smith, Elder, and Co.), 1858.

Dictionary of National Biography Papers Relating to Hostilities with Burma, presented [to Parliament] 15th March 1852, *c.*1940.

Further Papers Relating to Hostilities with Burma, presented [to Parliament] 15th March 1853, *c.* 1608.

Also consulted by the author were nineteenth century newspapers and magazines printed in British India and London: *The Bengal Hurkaru, The Bombay Gazette, The Englishman, The Madras Althenaeum, The Rangoon Gazette, The Times of India, The Graphic, The Illustrated London News* and *The Mirror*.

Select Burmese language texts:

Ba Yin, Hanthawaddy U, 'Pyitse hnin yanthu' [Property and the Enemy] *Myawaddy,* c. 1960, Rangoon.

Hla Thein, U, 'Myanmar Min Hlutdaw go Britisha do phyet thein pon' [The abolition of the Hlutdaw by the British], *Researches in Burmese History,* Rangoon (Department of Historical Research), 3, 1979.

____, 'Thibaw Min par daw ma mu mi thone hnit ah twin Aeingaleik-Myanmar set san ye' [The political situation between the British and the Burmese three years before the annexation] *Researches in Burmese History,* Rangoon (Department of Historical Research), 4, 1979.

Hman-nan maha ya-zawin-daw-gyi [The Glass Palace Chronicle]. 3 vols. Mandalay (Pyigyi-mandaing Press), 1967.

Kala, U, *Maha-ya-zawin-gyi* [The Great Royal Chronicle]. 3 vols. Rangoon (Hanthawaddy Press), 1962.

Kanni-myo-sar Minhtinyaza, *Mandalay Yadabon Maha ya-zawin daw-gyi* [History of Mandalay]. Edited by U Mg Mg Tin. Mandalay (Tetnaylin Press), 1969.

Kyan, Daw, 'Myanmar-pyi Aeindiya tha din sar myar e ah baw' [Comments by Indian Papers on the annexation of Burma] *Researches in Burmese History,* Rangoon, (Department of Historical Research), 1, 1977. [Burmese and English text.]

Man-yar-pyi [Mandalay Centenary Magazine], Mandalay (Mandalay Centenary Committee, 1959. [Numerous articles relating to the Mandalay period.]

Nan Nyunt Swe, 'Lay-se-khun-na-khu, Kulas myar tet se ka' [When the British came up in B.E.1247 (1885)], *Myawaddi, c.*1960, Rangoon.

Sann Thamein, *Myanmar-thuay, Myanmar-dah, Myanmar-sit-pyinna* [Burmese Blood, Burmese Sword and Burmese Art of War], Rangoon (Si-me-sar-pay), 1979.

Shwebo Mi Mi Gyi, Daw, *Min Let Wah* [Biography of Min Let Wah, minister to Mindon and Thibaw], Rangoon (Sarpaybeikman), 1979.

____, *Hle-thin-ah-twin Wun U Shwe Maung* [Biography of U Shwe Maung, Master of the Royal Barges to Mindon and Thibaw], Rangoon (Sarpaybeikman), 1985.

____, *Maha lu-ye-chun Shwepyi Wun U Pho Hlaing* [Biography of U Po Hlaing], Rangoon (Sarpaybeikman), 1995. [New information spanning five reigns.]

Sithu Aung, 'Bo-bwar ah-mway-ah-hnit Myanmar ah-pho-tan yadana myar..' [Precious stones, the heritage from our forefathers etc.,], *Loke-thar-pyi-thu* [Working People's Daily], 8 October 1991, Rangoon.

Taw Sein Ko, *Selections from the Records of the Hluttaw,* Rangoon (British Burma Press), 1926.

Tin, U Mg Mg, *Konbaungset Maha-ya-zawin-daw-gyi* [Chronicle of the Konbaung Dynasty: referred to in the text as *Konbaungset Chronicle*]. 3 vols. Rangoon (Laitimantaing Press), 1967.

Tin, Pagan U, *Myanmar min ok-chok-pon sadan* [Administration under the Burmese Kings]. 5 vols. Rangoon (Department of Culture), 1963-83.

Yi Yi, Dr, 'Lun khe thaw hnit ta yar ka Myanmar pyi' [Burma one hundred years ago] *Researches in Burmese History,* Rangoon (Department of Historical Research), 4, 1979.

Index

About the Author

Terence Blackburn was born in London in 1938. He joined the army and served in the Medical Corps for two years in Germany. Later, being attracted to work in health care, he was employed in a number of jobs in this field. His last position, before his early retirement, was as Senior Principal Administrative Officer at Guy's Hospital in London.

He became interested in the history and culture of Burma through his acquaintence with the Burmese art historian, author and painter, Noel F. Singer. Accompanying Singer on endless forays to antique markets and auction houses since the early 1960s also sharpened his curiosity in things Burmese. Blackburn has never been to Burma because of his dislike of flying, so it is perhaps fortunate that his period of interest is the nineteenth century, as much of the material is in the United Kingdom.

He found time to locate the majority of the enormous number of Burmese objects held in many of the museums and institutes in the United Kingdom, Europe and America. Over one thousand museums were involved in this extensively researched private survey which took more than five years to complete. The results are to be found in *A Report on the Location of Burmese Artifacts in Museums*, published in 1994 in the Kiscadale Asia Research series.

Blackburn's fascination with the Anglo Burmese Wars and his delight in finding inconsistancies between official accounts, newspaper reports and the correspondence from participants and observers on the spot, gave him encouragement to write the present work.